JARED'S STORY

JARED'S STORY
A Boy in a Bubble and How His Family Saved His Life

BARRY REISMAN

Crown Publishers, Inc.   **New York**

To my wife, Marlene, with love

362.1
Rei

Inquiries should be addressed to Crown Publishers, Inc., One Park Avenue, New York, New York 10016

Printed in the United States of America

Published simultaneously in Canada by General Publishing Company Limited

Library of Congress Cataloging in Publication Data

Reisman, Barry.
  Jared's story.

  1. Reisman, Jared. 2. Pediatric allergy—Patients—United States—Biography. I. Title.
RJ386.R45R45 1984   362.1′9892′97   84-17501
ISBN 0-517-55423-2

10 9 8 7 6 5 4 3 2 1

First Edition

Designed by David Connolly

Contents

Illustrations follow page 90.

Acknowledgments

I owe a special debt of thanks to the three people who helped make this book possible:

To my wife, Marlene, for her advice, encouragement, and support throughout the writing of the manuscript.

To Karyn Feiden, my editor at Crown, whose suggestions for organizing and elaborating the material helped make this book a reality.

To Marjorie Fishman Beggs for her most valued editorial services, which put the manuscript into final literary form.

I

Our Son, the Boy in a Bubble

1

Plunging into the Nightmare

This is the story of a little boy who lost his right to live. He can no longer see a doctor, attend school with other children, or receive a religious education. His only right is to an institution and death without dignity. His crime: He survived an illness so debilitating that it was diagnosed, incorrectly, as severe retardation. The agony and the limitations placed on him continue to this day.

Ironically, he lost these rights under the law, through the very laws that were meant to protect the rights of all handicapped children and guarantee them an education. Under these laws, the state of California assumes a major responsibility in the care of these children. But these laws, as well meaning as they may be, leave room for abuse in cases of misdiagnoses. The laws' power to place children in institutions can have two negative effects: It can deny them a normal education and it can cover up and perpetuate a misdiagnosis.

This story is true—it happened to our son Jared. And, incredibly, it happened in twentieth-century America. Given the same circumstances, it could happen to anyone's child. Thousands of children are misdiagnosed each year. We hope that, by telling our story, perhaps we can bring pressure on the authorities to enact legislation that will reduce the chances for the abuse of the law, and so spare Jared—and all children who have been the innocent victims of a sometimes flawed system—further suffering.

Jared today is a talkative twelve-year-old filled with love for life. Everything he does is full of gusto: eating his favorite meal, pedaling his exercise bike, writing a humorous composition, programming our home computer. He moves and speaks quickly and radiates a spirit that's a joy to behold. It's almost as if he knows life's a gift and he's going to make the most of every moment. His exuberance is contagious.

There's also a serious side to Jared. He's loving and compassionate, sensitive to the feelings of others. He asks why there are wars, why kids get hooked on drugs, why there is so much crime. Like most children his age, he views the world through innocent eyes and wonders why it is filled with the kind of suffering he sees on TV news all the time and how it all can be stopped.

On the brink of adolescence, Jared seems ready to leave his little-boy days behind. He's started talking about high school, dating, college, and choosing a career. We're proud of him, and, like all parents, we hope our son will find his way into the adult world holding on to the same good spirits he's shown throughout his childhood.

Jared's story has an ordinary beginning. On a hot Sacramento afternoon, August 15, 1972, my wife, Marlene, called me at work: "Barry, I'm at the obstetrician's—he says I'm in labor. Could you meet me at the hospital?"

"Great, yes, I'll leave right now!" Driving there, I was thinking that the baby had picked a convenient time to come and that Marlene had breezed through this pregnancy with no complications and with minimal weight gain.

At the hospital, a nurse quickly handed me gown, booties, and mask. I struggled into them, all thumbs, then dashed into the delivery room where the doctor was preparing for the birth.

"When does the pain start?" Marlene asked the doctor a few minutes later.

"It's almost over," he answered. He and the nurses started laughing. Then Jared emerged— beautiful, alert and healthy, a full-term baby, eight pounds, eight ounces. He gave a lusty cry.

"That's a good pair of lungs," the doctor said to him, "but what are you crying about?"

"Maybe he knows we wanted a girl."

"Or he doesn't like that you bought him dresses,"

the doctor joked. He declared Jared in perfect condition. Marlene and I hugged and kissed each other, delighted with this, our second child, and thrilled with how healthy he was.

Four and a half years before, our son David had been born with both a heart defect and hyaline membrane disease, a condition, usually fatal then, in which the lungs fail to expand properly at birth. The 80 percent oxygen given to keep David alive for his first two weeks of life threatened to leave him blind —oxygen levels above 40 percent can destroy a newborn's retinas. But expert care saved David. When Jared was born, David was perfectly healthy and normal.

Marlene says the days in the hospital after Jared's birth were among the happiest of her life. Jared was very responsive—his pediatrician pronounced him "about the most alert newborn I've seen."

Just a few hours after his birth, Jared was brought into Marlene's room so she could feed him. He started drinking from his bottle, but then he turned his head and saw Marlene for the first time. He stopped drinking and stared at her, fascinated it seemed. His alertness thrilled Marlene.

On the day Marlene and Jared came home from the hospital, David, who'd told us he had always wanted a brother, greeted them bashfully. He followed Marlene when she carried Jared to his crib. But when she turned to give David a hug, he yelled, "Don't touch me! I feel hate!" He turned away, his face white.

"Who do you hate?" Marlene asked.

"You and that baby!" David screamed as he ran into his room.

Marlene tried to comfort him, but he wouldn't let her. Later that night, when she went to read him a bedtime story, he perked up. "Are you still going to read to me every night, Mommy?"

"Well, of course. We'll do everything just like before."

When he was convinced he wouldn't be displaced, David returned to his normal, cheerful self. The next day he went off to nursery school and, according to his teacher, announced proudly, "I've got a new brother."

Jared grew quickly into a bright and outgoing infant, eager to explore everything around him. By five months, he could pull himself up to a standing position, and by nine months he was walking. At a year he showed astute mechanical abilities, putting together puzzles rapidly and spending hours playing with manipulative toys. At the same age he started saying a few words. We have a tape of Jared and David playing together when Jared was fifteen months. On it Jared is communicating clearly in one-word sentences—"blanket . . . bottle . . . David . . . blocks . . ."

Marlene and I remember Jared between fifteen and eighteen months as a vibrant boy playing tirelessly in our yard, well-coordinated, running gracefully in big strides like an athlete. He learned to ride his tricycle, and he and David would race down the sidewalk, Jared pedaling furiously, trying to keep up with David on his trainer bike.

Sacramento is a wonderful place to raise children; the house we'd bought four years before was perfect for our growing family. It is a California ranch-style, custom-built to the owners' specifications six years before we bought it. All the rooms, including the three bedrooms and three baths, are spacious. The family room has a beam ceiling, wood-paneled walls, and a large brick fireplace and hearth. A full glass wall with sliding doors overlooks a screened-in patio and beautifully landscaped back-yard. Outside, the heavy wood-shake roof and exterior blend in with the many trees on the lot. And though the house is on a quiet circle away from traffic, it is close to shopping, schools, and the free-way.

Those were happy times for all of us. Life had been good, and we were grateful. Marlene and I loved to sit outside the house, watching our little boys play noisily, and talking about when we were kids ourselves—I, in New York City and Marlene, in North Dakota—and about our six married years together before we'd started a family.

Ever since I'd been a small boy, I'd dreamed of moving to California. Fresh out of college, with a BS degree in chemical engineering from Carnegie Tech in Pittsburgh, I felt pretty lucky when I landed a job with the Aerojet General Corporation in Sacramento. It was the early sixties, and there was a lot of excitement at Aerojet in those days. It had some big contracts for building liquid and solid rockets, like *Polaris* and *Minuteman.* The first *Sputnik* had gone up a few years before, and the U.S. space program had accelerated. At work there was much excited talk about man someday walking in space and eventually going to the moon.

My first job at Aerojet was as a quality control engineer, designing inspection procedures for solid rocket motors and propellants. The work included design analysis of critical components for quality improvement, geared to ensuring that the rockets being produced were reliable and failsafe. My job was challenging and rewarding, and I remember that, when President Kennedy ushered in the space age and told all Americans how important it was, I felt proud to be part of the space race.

Life in Sacramento was agreeable, too, everything I'd expected California to be—year-round good weather and an easy-going life-style. Sacramento had a small-town flavor, with none of the fast pace of a large city. Yet, just a ninety-mile drive to the west were all the attractions and culture of San Francisco. Plenty to do there for a young, unmarried guy. And a two-hour drive to the east were the Sierra Nevada mountains, including Lake Tahoe, with year-round activities like fishing, hiking, camping, even gambling, and, in winter, cross-country skiing.

A few months after I moved to Sacramento I met Marlene, then a college sophomore, at a swimming party given by a mutual friend. The temperature that day had hit 110 degrees. I remember my first sight of Marlene—tall, slender, with long blond hair, blue eyes, full face. I was smitten instantly.

I rushed over to introduce myself, and soon we were absorbed in sharing backgrounds and interests. By the time the evening temperature had cooled down, I'd asked Marlene for our first date. Even on that night, I knew she was going to be someone special in my life.

We were married two years later and quickly

settled into married life. She was majoring in psychology and physiology at Sacramento State University. Among Marlene's friends, I was affectionately known as "the guy putting Marlene through college." She was a conscientious student. I remember a couple of her professors saying they hoped she'd be able to go on to graduate or medical school.

Private flying was a common interest Marlene and I shared in our early married years. California's mild climate, sunny skies, and many general aviation airports made it a private pilot's heaven. We belonged to a private flying club, where a warm camaraderie between the pilots meant many a weekend spent sharing flying experiences. We used to joke, "When two pilots meet, there goes the whole afternoon."

On weekends Marlene and I took leisurely, cross-country flights to nearby resort areas in our rented Cessna 150. She was taking flying lessons and had passed the written exam, so she navigated those trips. There is something idyllic about the relaxation of flying. Looking down at the earth, all cares seem to dissipate and there is an exhilarating feeling of freedom.

Now, with our young family, Marlene and I had little time for flying, but life was very good. We often talked about how contented we were, how the boys were growing, how well everything was going.

We didn't know it then, but we were about to be plunged into a nightmare that would last for years.

When Jared was one and a half, we took a family trip to Disneyland. David had been asking to go there for some time, but we'd postponed the trip, waiting until Jared was old enough to enjoy it. On the car trip down to Anaheim, the weather turned cool and wet. We drove past Disneyland that evening before checking into a motel, and at the sight of the bright lights, the Monorail, the Matterhorn, in the distance, the two sleepy boys in the back seat suddenly perked up, enthralled. That night they were so antsy we could hardly get them to bed.

The next day we gathered our rain gear and drove over to Disneyland. We couldn't have picked a worse day if we'd tried: It was crowded, the lines were long, at times the cold drizzle turned into a downpour, and we had to stop going on rides and stand huddled under an umbrella. We did manage to see a few of the attractions, and the boys were having a good time, but the weather was so unpleasant, we cut the trip short and drove home the next day.

David was starting to sniffle. By the time we got home, Jared had a cold, too. David's cold went away after a week, but Jared's grew worse and developed into a strange persistent illness.

His lips swelled and mucus ran profusely from his nose. His eyes watered and were sensitive to light. Worst of all, a pounding pain in his head made it impossible for him to lie down to sleep. Marlene had to hold him and comfort him late into the night until he fell asleep, his face contorted in a vain effort to ease the pain. When he woke in the morning, his eyelids were glued shut with mucus, mucus covered his bed and the floor of his room.

When Jared didn't get well, Marlene called his pediatrician. He said it just sounded like a bad cold and recommended that we keep Jared warm, give him plenty of liquids, and not bring him in for an office visit: "There are just more germs here he could catch. He's better off at home."

Jared's symptoms continued. We certainly were concerned about him, but we weren't alarmed. The doctor had reassured us that it was a nasty cold, possibly flu, and it was going to take a while to go away. In the meantime, we tried to take good care of him so his condition wouldn't turn into something worse, like pneumonia. But after four more weeks of it, Jared wasn't getting any better. He seemed to be deaf. He stopped talking. Marlene finally called the pediatrician and made an appointment for a checkup.

Jared's pediatrician was a relaxed, mild-mannered man in his late forties, in whom we had the utmost confidence. Despite a small crowded office, he always took time to answer all our questions. His diagnosis after examining Jared was "a bad cold combined with teething," and he prescribed aspirin and a teething ring.

"But Jared seems to have lost his hearing, and he's stopped talking," we protested. The pediatrician carefully examined Jared's ears with an otoscope. "They look perfectly fine to me," he said. "I'm sure he'll start talking again as soon as he feels better."

Driving home, Marlene and I agreed we both felt relieved by the diagnosis. We trusted the pediatrician and had no reason to doubt his medical opinion.

The teething ring and aspirin didn't help at all. Jared still had a blinding pain in his head and excessive mucus. He didn't talk and didn't seem to hear.

We had long talks with friends and relatives, describing our feelings of helplessness, and though they gave us comfort and opinions about Jared's long-running illness, no one knew how to help him feel better.

Marlene's parents were incredibly supportive and eased many of our fears. They were pillars of strength I'd leaned on more than once in the many years I'd known them.

I'd met them soon after Marlene and I started dating and felt comfortable with them at once. Like my own parents, they had a European background. At our first meeting, I learned that Marlene's mother was born in southern Russia near the Caspian Sea, while her father's parents had emigrated from Gottland, an island in the Baltic Sea that belongs to Sweden. I told them my mother's parents came from Russia and my father from Warsaw, and we started swapping stories on everything from foods to the Russian Revolution. Also, like my parents, I found Marlene's family stressed the work ethic and deeply appreciated the freedom they found here. That's something children of immigrants seem to share. We don't take life for granted.

Marlene and I had a year-long courtship before we got engaged. After the anouncement, my father, a retired businessman, came to California from New York to meet Marlene and her parents, and was so pleased to have Marlene in the family, he gave her a two-and-a-half-carat diamond ring, a family heirloom.

Marlene never got to meet my beloved mother,

who passed away from lupus erythematosus shortly after our engagement. I know Mom would have liked Marlene. They were so much alike, both so kind and compassionate.

I have other things to regret. My dad and, of course, Marlene's parents were thrilled when we finally announced that our first child was on the way. It saddens me to this day that Dad never knew about the birth of the first grandchild he'd so anxiously awaited.

Marlene and I had just rented a large Tudor-style house in the Oakland hills. Marlene's pregnancy was easy, and she was able to keep up her busy schedule, continuing graduate school and taking flying lessons. Like many parents-to-be, we had no idea how this child would change our lives. Then, on December 22, 1967, a little less than two months before the baby was due, Marlene went into premature labor. A few hours later David was born, and I noticed at once that something was wrong with him. His chest was palpitating rapidly, as he desperately tried to breathe. Later that day I got the bleak news about David's heart defect and hyaline membrane disease.

Two days later the doctor called to say David's lungs weren't getting any better, and he was losing weight because he could be fed only intravenous fluids. Marlene came home, but every day we went to the hospital to see David. We stood looking through the glass partition, watching him struggle to breathe, and we knew even then he was a real fighter. We didn't know how long he'd be with us, so every day at the hospital was precious to us.

I'd been off work for nine days—who could concentrate under such conditions? On the ninth day, the doctor explained the high oxygen dose being given to keep David alive threatened to leave him blind. We were torn apart, not knowing if it was better for our baby to live or die. We spent that day crying and praying, but we knew that, even if he was blind, we wanted David to live. We weren't going to let the hopelessness get us. If David was struggling to live, he needed parents who would love and wait for him. That afternoon, we went to a toy store and bought him his first toys, mobiles and a rattle. As long as he was alive, we were going to treat him like any other baby.

When we got home from the toy store, I could hear the phone ringing even before I opened the door. It was the hospital, I was sure, and I rushed to the phone. But, over my racing heart, I heard a strange voice from far away identifying himself as my father's doctor. My dad had just passed away—a sudden stroke. By now, I was in such a state of shock, I was barely able to comprehend what was happening.

As our pediatrician had suggested, because of Dad's heart condition, I hadn't told him about David's birth or his life struggle. We were waiting for David to improve. I always felt Dad was cheated in not knowing he had a grandson. The irony was that, just a few days after Dad's funeral, David miraculously began to recover. When we brought David home a week later, I thought about Dad's life passing and David's being spared. I cried, not knowing, but accepting. Perhaps it had been a trade-off under God's infinite wisdom.

2

Respite and Relapse

Jared was now twenty-four months old, and still he had his enigmatic "cold." Then, suddenly and mysteriously, he was back to his old frisky self. We were thrilled, sure his illness was behind us. For three weeks, family life returned to normal.

It was a short respite. Jared had a new relapse, and all his symptoms were worse than the first time.

The scenario kept repeating—long sick periods followed by two- to three-week well periods. When he was well, with all his swelling, pain, and heavy mucus discharge gone, he'd pick up where he left off. His appetite would return, he'd sleep long hours, he'd start playing with his toys again. However, he still seemed deaf and didn't try to talk. We figured he'd start again after he'd been well for a while longer.

Jared's relapses almost always started when he was outdoors, in the park or the yard. He'd walk a few feet, then suddenly stretch out his arms, his head tilted to one side. Looking like he was drunk, he'd stagger, then fall helplessly to the ground. Determined, he'd pick himself up, only to fall down again. Marlene usually carried him into the house, and soon after the crippling headaches, high fever, continuous mucus discharge would follow. At night we could hear his desperate efforts to breathe.

Now every time Jared had a relapse, Marlene became very frightened. She'd call the pediatrician, but he didn't seem alarmed. Marlene had the feeling, she says, that the pediatrician thought she was exaggerating Jared's symptoms. When she was overcome with fear and did take Jared to the pediatrician, he told her Jared was probably having another bad bout with the flu and was just too sick to walk. His theory, he told her, was that David was bringing home cold and flu germs from kindergarten. It seemed there was nothing we could do but hope and pray Jared would soon build up his immunity to those germs. We even considered taking David out of school.

During the next few months, Marlene's devotion and perseverance were put to the test over and over. I know I wouldn't have been able to endure the long, sleepless hours she spent caring for Jared. She gave her time unselfishly, never complaining.

As I watched her keep going, day after day, my mind flashed back to the time when she was pregnant with David. Her girlfriends had thrown a baby shower, and when I came home from work that day, the last of her friends were leaving. Joni, her best friend from college, took me aside at the front door: "Marlene's going to be a great mother. You'll see."

I didn't think a lot about her pronouncement then. I just took it as a nice compliment. But the remark proved prophetic, and I've thought of it a million times since.

I couldn't help Marlene with Jared during the day. I had a full-time, demanding job as an air pollution engineer for the California Air Resources Board. Air pollution engineering was an exciting new field at the time. The public's increased awareness of the harmful effects of industrial and motor pollution had resulted in passage of the federal Clean Air Act, and California was in the forefront of implementing tough, clean-air standards. Air monitoring stations had been set up throughout the state to measure pollutant levels. My department and my colleagues and I were responsible for establishing the procedures field workers would use to measure those pollutants, and we also checked the accuracy of the sophisticated, state-of-the-art, electronic measuring instruments themselves to assure that only valid data were collected.

But, despite my heavy work load during the weekdays, I helped Marlene as much as I could in the evenings and on weekends, cleaning the house, cooking, attending to David.

David, in the meantime, was taking everything matter-of-factly. He seemed unfazed by Jared's illness and just kept waiting for him to get well again, so they could start playing.

After a year of trying to survive like this, we were desperate. Our entire family life revolved around Jared's illness, and he wasn't getting any better. Somehow I managed to get through the ordeal of Jared's illness without disrupting my work. Family sick leave and vacation took care of the times when I was needed at home. And my colleagues were very accommodating, not scheduling extended out-of-town business trips, knowing that in an emergency I might be needed at home. Their understanding continued throughout Jared's on-again, off-again troubles, which we endured for so many, many months.

We kept taking him back to the pediatrician, who kept assuring us there was nothing to be alarmed about, that Jared would someday outgrow his problem. We were encouraged by Jared's good spells, and we wanted the doctor's diagnosis to be true, so we continued to believe him.

But new and terrifying symptoms developed when Jared was two and a half. One evening, Marlene was getting him ready for his bath when she saw that his chest, back, arms, and legs were covered with black-and-blue marks. She'd been with him all day and was sure he hadn't fallen or injured himself. What was happening? Then, every day during his bath, she'd notice new marks. She pressed on the bruises to see if they were tender, but Jared didn't respond. He didn't even seem to notice them.

One day Jared cut his finger slightly while playing with a toy. It began to bleed profusely. Marlene tried desperately to stop the bleeding by wrapping bandages and finally a cloth tightly around it. But every time she removed them, the tiny cut still bled. A terrifying thought hit her: Leukemia—that's why he's bruising so easily. She ran to the phone and called the pediatrician. "Bring him right now," he said.

For the first time, the pediatrician seemed concerned about all of Jared's strange symptoms. Were there any incidences of hemophilia in our families? Did we remember any of our grandparents mentioning a distant relative with the disease? As far as we knew, we said, our family histories were free of hemophilia. The doctor still suspected the disease and ordered a series of blood tests for both hemophilia and leukemia.

For two days we waited fearfully for the results of the blood tests. When the results came in, the pediatrician phoned immediately: "Jared doesn't have either disease. He really had me worried for a while!" He admitted he was puzzled by Jared's symptoms, but added, "At this point, I don't think there's cause for any great concern."

Jared's illness continued, sometimes severe, sometimes less so. We began to notice that, when we took him to an air-conditioned restaurant or indoor shopping mall, his symptoms subsided and he became more alert. Marlene often took him to a nearby restaurant so he could eat comfortably.

We tried a trip to Fort Bragg, a resort area on the northern California coast, hoping the clear ocean air would give Jared the same kind of relief he got in the restaurant. In the car, he was nearly delirious, and by the time we arrived at the cabin, he was in such pain he went wild. His face, eyelids, and lips were swollen grotesquely and mucus poured from his nose. He tried to run out of the cabin to escape the pain, so we called the manager to help us lock the windows and pushed a dresser in front of the door. Frustrated and desperate, Jared took a fireplace poker and chased us with it. We were terrified—Jared seemed to be losing his mind. And David, usually cool, was so upset he fled into one of the bedrooms of the cabin and stayed there all night. We finally relented and took Jared for a walk along the beach. There he calmed down. We took turns that night on the beach with Jared and left for home the next morning.

Two months later, Jared had another remission period. He still couldn't hear or talk, but he was obviously happy about feeling better. He got playful and especially loved visiting his grandmother, who lives a few blocks away. They'd play rough-and-tumble games, and she'd give him endless piggyback rides.

To celebrate Jared's third birthday, we took the children to Marine World, an aquatic amusement park south of San Francisco. Jared was feeling fine, squealing with delight as a whale hurled himself into the air and splashed water on the grandstand watchers. When we toured the aquarium, Jared led Marlene excitedly through the aisles, pointing to every fish behind the giant glass enclosures.

On the way home, we took a little detour and drove through our old neighborhood in the Oakland hills, where we had lived until David was three and a half. Then, as we were driving through downtown Berkeley, David spotted a bus and yelled, "Let's take a bus ride! I've never been on a bus." It sounded like fun, so I parked the car, and we all climbed on a crowded bus. The moment it started rolling, Jared began jumping up and down, giggling, acting like it was an amusement park ride. The passengers were all smiles, watching the ebullient Jared. None of them would have guessed this happy little boy had just spent the last year struggling for his life.

Later, Jared ate a hearty dinner and throughout the day had acted so normal and grown-up, we had new hope that his "terrible twos" and illness were over. We had another child on the way, and we were hoping for the daughter we had always wanted.

Jared stayed well for many weeks, and our family life gradually returned to normal. I started actively gardening again, a love I share with Marlene's mother, who has spent a lifetime cultivating fruits and vegetables in her large backyard.

On weekends, she and I went poking around nurseries, usually coming home with a carload of plants. We started trying our luck at growing exotic fruits like kiwi and guava. Our dream was to someday have an enormous banquet where we'd serve huge baskets of homegrown fruits with special wines. My mother-in-law loves to cook and would always jump at the chance to prepare my favorite foods—cabbage soup, potato pirogen, and piroshki. With Jared better, I could be much more appreciative of her efforts.

Those returns to normalcy were rejuvenating and gave me new mental and physical strength for the hard times that would come again when Jared was sick.

It was searing hot that summer, so Jared spent most of his time inside our air-conditioned house. He seemed so much better, we decided to enroll him in a nursery school, a lovely place located in a heavily wooded area.

He came home after the first day of school feeling sick. By the end of the week, all his old symptoms were back. His teacher called Marlene in and told her she felt Jared was very ill and needed medical attention before he could continue school. She also suggested we have Jared's hearing checked. She suspected he was completely deaf. Another teacher at the school who had worked with deaf children had tried to check Jared's hearing by clapping her hands and ringing a bell behind his back. He hadn't responded at all.

The pediatrician examined Jared once more and found his ears impacted with wax and filled with fluid. "I think it's allergies," he said. "I didn't really suspect it sooner since your family history is allergy-free." He referred us to the allergy section of a large medical clinic, noted for its excellent diagnostic and treatment facilities. There we were assigned an allergist, a soft-spoken woman in her forties with a motherly touch.

The allergist ordered a complete physical examination and a battery of tests. Small amounts of various pollens and other allergens were put on Jared's skin and then pinpricks were made through them. A red itchy swelling in the pinprick area would indicate a positive reaction. Jared tested positive to almost all airborne substances—pollen, dust, dander, and mold.

What the allergist recommended was a three-fold approach in treating Jared: desensitization shots, medication, and a dust-free environment, especially in his bedroom. We had to clean the house thoroughly, get rid of anything containing animal fibers such as wool rugs, strip Jared's room of everything that collected dust, including carpets, curtains, upholstered furniture, and books, and replace them with nonallergenic items. Marlene, she said, should wet-mop his room daily.

Also recommended were weekly shots and doses of antihistamines and decongestants, to control the allergy symptoms. She said the shots, if successful, would give Jared lasting relief by building up his natural immunity to the allergens. Beginning with minute amounts of allergens diluted in a saline solution, the doses and the time between injections would be increased gradually. We understood the treatment could take months, even years, but we decided to go ahead with it because it seemed the only hope for Jared.

Jared started weekly allergy shots and antihistamines and decongestants, and he reacted immediately and violently to them. Not only did his original symptoms return, they got progressively worse. His coordination failed, he stumbled and fell, he lost his appetite. Once, after taking only a quarter-teaspoon of antihistamine, he became delirious and slept for thirty-six hours.

The next year was one of the most miserable of Jared's young life. When he was on allergy shots and medication, he fell apart completely and acted like a hyperactive wild animal. We sometimes had to tie him down in his crib at night. He didn't seem to know what was going on around him. He would thrash around helplessly, sick, unresponsive to our efforts to comfort him. We kept returning to the allergist, who told us to continue the shots. We did.

And, with each injection and dose of medicine, Jared became worse. Finally, one of the shots nearly put him into convulsions.

Ever since he'd been on shots and medication, in the back of our minds, we'd had a fear that Jared might not make it through the treatment. We were torn between the allergy treatment that was making him sicker—but that the doctors said could help him —and our deep instinct that the treatment was more risky than the illness itself.

We also knew there was an aspect of the illness not explained by allergies alone: bleeding episodes, bruising easily, and intolerance to medicines. Now, when Jared went into convulsions, our worst fears were confirmed—the whole course of events was life-threatening.

We rushed him to the emergency room of a nearby hospital in the middle of the night. The doctor on duty listened to his history and suggested we stop the treatment. He was sympathetic, reassuring us Jared might someday outgrow his allergies. "Don't give up," he said. "Remember, Jared was a healthy baby." Jared's health did improve when we stopped the shots and the medication.

It was a much-needed reprieve. Marlene was in her last few weeks of a difficult pregnancy. The month before, her obstetrician began suspecting triplets and ordered x-rays, but they had to be postponed because Marlene had the flu. A few weeks later, the doctors changed the diagnosis to twins and took x-rays that, to our great relief, revealed one unusually large baby.

Unlike Jared, Alicia was born in the middle of the night. She was in a breech position and had to be delivered by Caesarean section, and I, for the first time, had to sweat it out in the waiting room with other distraught, expectant fathers. I felt uncomfortable and helpless, not allowed to be with Marlene to welcome our child into the world.

Two hours after Marlene went in for surgery, a smiling nurse emerged from the operating room carrying a tiny bundle.

"You have a daughter," she said, "and your wife's doing fine."

"Is it a boy or a girl?" I asked, dazed.

"It's a girl," she laughed. "Here she is."

I could hardly believe it—we had the daughter we'd always wanted! I called Marlene's parents right away to tell them the good news. Then, exhausted but thrilled, I drove home and got there just in time to wake eight-year-old David for school and tell him he had the sister he'd been waiting for and Mom was fine. He managed a grin though half asleep: "A sister!"

We knew David had been worried about Marlene and the baby during the pregnancy because he'd confided his fears to his third-grade teacher. She helped him through the waiting period by praying for Marlene and the baby every day during school chapel. David also was helped by his grandfather who took him to and from school during Marlene's pregnancy. They had long talks that David told us were "great."

Three-year-old Jared was thrilled when Marlene and Alicia came home from the hospital. That first day he stood over the bassinet, staring at her. She moved, and he jumped back, startled, and started to laugh—the "doll" in the bassinet was real. He reached in and gently stroked her head and hands.

Alicia was a good baby from the start and slept long hours. Both boys adored her. David would come home from school and carry her back and forth through the house, talking and singing to her. Jared grew so attached to her that he'd cry whenever Marlene took her to her grandmother's house for the day.

After a few untroubled weeks, Jared's symptoms returned. The allergist urged us to continue trying different medications, in the hope one would finally work. That the medications actually intensified the symptoms they were supposed to relieve baffled us, but we kept trying. Every antihistamine and decongestant on the market, prescription and over-the-counter, made his symptoms worse and created serious side effects that lasted for as long as three weeks. We waited and hoped for new medicines that would help Jared. They never did.

Finally, out of sheer desperation, we stopped all the medications. I described Jared's reaction to medication to our local pharmacist, who felt the reaction was highly unusual and theorized that he might have a metabolic disorder that kept him from breaking down drugs properly. I called another pharmacist at

Camarillo State Hospital. He agreed with that theory and thought perhaps Jared might be missing a liver substance that breaks down such chemicals. This, he said, also might explain why medication that lasted only a few hours in most people persisted for weeks in Jared. But he didn't know how anyone could prove this theory.

Jared's hearing grew worse, and he still wasn't talking. We'd taken Jared to have his hearing tested at a clinic, and the exam showed he had no nerve conduction in one ear—that is, he was technically deaf in that ear. Another ear doctor theorized that Jared's allergies were affecting his inner ears, disturbing his balance and coordination, and causing periods of total deafness. Now we decided to take Jared back to his pediatrician once again. "Chronic otitis media" was his diagnosis, a painful buildup of fluid in the ears, caused by allergies. He referred us to an ear specialist.

The ear specialist, who occupied a large, plush office, was a tall, well-dressed man with an authoritative manner. He examined Jared and found permanent damage in the middle ears.

To prevent further damage, the specialist wanted to put tubes in Jared's ears to drain off the fluid, a procedure known as myringotomy. It involves making a small incision in the eardrum and inserting a slender ventilation tube to allow drainage of the middle ear. The surgery is done under anesthesia, and the patient has to take four teaspoons of antihistamines before surgery to dry up the mucous membranes. When we told the doctor about Jared's reaction to even the smallest amount of medication, he declined to operate. He didn't think Jared would live through the operation. "I don't treat dying children," he said.

What a cold and callous way to tell parents their child was dying! The remark made us so angry, we wanted to grab Jared and get him away from this doctor as quickly as possible.

Before we stumbled out of his office, he recommended that we take Jared to the Mayo Clinic, and he gave us a referral. As horrible as the situation was, his referral gave us some relief, since we knew Mayo was the top of the mountain when it came to medical care. Maybe the doctors there could help save Jared.

We decided to consult another allergist before committing ourselves to the long and desperate trip to the Mayo Clinic. This allergist, in his early thirties, occupied a large but sparsely furnished office. His demeanor was calm and sympathetic. He said he suspected Jared's problem was caused by something more than allergies, that perhaps the diagnosis was incomplete, but that he didn't know how to deal with it. He told us about a similar situation he had faced with his own four-year-old son, who had been diagnosed as having leukemia and was scheduled for chemotherapy. "I really suspected an error in the diagnosis because he had gotten sick so suddenly. So I took him out of town to a university medical center. They found he'd been poisoned by insecticides." His son was treated and made a complete recovery, he said. "These are difficult cases. They need a kind of expertise that's not available around here, only at university hospitals or large medical centers like the Mayo Clinic."

As we were leaving, the allergist mentioned having seen a television movie called *The Boy in the Bubble*. John Travolta played a teenage boy with an immune deficiency who lived in a plastic bubble isolator. The allergist thought perhaps a chamber of purified air might help Jared, but he didn't know if such a device was available. In any case, he suggested we watch the movie the next evening, when it was rerun. We were intrigued by the idea, but we didn't think much more about it. At the time, it seemed like science fiction.

3

The Mayo Clinic

A long 2,000-mile road trip to the Mayo Clinic in Rochester, Minnesota, lay ahead of us. Because of Jared's ear problems, we couldn't risk an airplane trip—the change in cabin pressure might have ruptured his eardrums.

As we drove away from the house that morning, David stood at the window crying. Leaving three-month-old Alicia and David behind was painful, even though we knew Marlene's mother would give them the best of care. Our trip was something we just had to do for Jared.

The drive through the Sierra Nevadas—twisting mountain roads with altitudes up to 7,200 feet—was hard on Jared. Marlene and I were worried about his steadily weakening condition, and I was finding it harder and harder to stay within the speed limit. Just before we reached Nevada, I saw a highway patrol car, sirens blaring, coming up fast behind me. I pulled over to the shoulder.

"You were exceeding the speed limit," the officer said. "May I see your license?"

"I'm sorry, I didn't realize I was going so fast. My son's very sick, and we're taking him to the Mayo Clinic in Minnesota."

When the officer bent down to look in the back seat and saw Jared, pale and listless, he handed back my license. "It looks like you have enough troubles. Just take it slower from now on."

About thirty minutes later, I was stopped again. This time, two officers came over to our car and told me to get out. Shaking, I opened the door.

"What's the problem?" one of them asked.

"Our son's very sick. We're taking him to the Mayo Clinic."

He asked for my license, car registration, and proof that we were indeed going to the Mayo Clinic. I handed them over. I wasn't let go quite so easily this time. The officers went back to their car to look over the papers for what seemed an eternity. I sat in the car, white, still shaking, wondering what they'd do to me.

Finally one officer came back. "Under the circumstances, I won't cite you, but I'm giving you a warning that I've recorded."

I thanked him and told him I'd never gotten a speeding ticket. For the rest of the trip, I kept a careful eye on the speedometer.

At Reno, we stopped for lunch at a casino restaurant. Jared was so weak, he couldn't eat. His face fell into the plate of food the waitress set before him. Marlene and I sat there, the color rising in our faces. We could see we were making the other diners uncomfortable; they kept trying to avoid looking at Jared. So we paid the bill and left.

When we got to Nebraska, Jared was starting to feel better. That night we stayed in Grand Island, and for the first time on the trip, Jared took his own shower and dressed himself. He walked around the motel room, curiously inspecting the furniture, the pictures on the wall, the TV, and by the time we reached the rolling farmlands of Iowa the next day, Jared had really perked up. He loved the dairy herds grazing in the pastures, the long grain trains roaring by, the peaceful small towns. Several times he motioned excitedly for us to turn back so he could get another look at the animals or a tiny town. Marlene and I were caught up in his excitement, seeing the scenery like new through Jared's eyes. We stopped often.

On the fourth day, we reached Rochester and checked into a motel near the clinic. Jared was feeling so much better, we knew he could be examined as an outpatient, and that was a relief. Had he remained sick, he probably would have had to be hospitalized.

The staff at the clinic were relaxed and friendly but baffled by Jared's symptoms. His assigned pediatrician in the allergy department scheduled him for three days of extensive testing: x-rays, skin tests for allergies, blood tests, RAST antigen tests, and an audiogram. Because of the risk of convulsions, the pediatrician decided not to run the tests on those allergens to which Jared had previously shown a highly allergic reaction. And when the audiologist found Jared to be totally deaf, he discontinued the examination and set up an appointment with the chief ear surgeon.

Jared didn't cry once during all the tests. Between tests he played happily with the toys in the examining room like any three-year-old boy. On our last day at the clinic, we consulted with the pediatrician. She suspected severe allergies, she said, but couldn't make a final diagnosis until all the test results were in, possibly as long as six weeks. Though we knew we'd have to wait more than a month for an answer, we left the Mayo Clinic feeling optimistic that Jared's illness would be diagnosed and hoping it could be treated.

Jared was still feeling better on the trip home from the Mayo Clinic, so traveling was easier. We did notice, however, that after we passed Nebraska, his nose started to run and his face swelled. We realized the reverse had happened at the same point on the trip east. Like an imaginary "dateline," east was good for Jared, west was bad. But he made it through the Sierra Nevadas without getting too sick.

At home, Jared and his grandmother had a reunion filled with hugs, kisses, and tears. Jared seemed to be entering one of his well periods, and all of us were feeling pretty good.

But, when the call came from the pediatrician, inviting us back for a follow-up visit, the news was worse than any so far. She said the clinic could find no identifiable disease or disorder and speculated that Jared was suffering from a one-of-a-kind illness, possibly an immunological disorder, and might not live past the age of eight. Still, she encouraged us to come back to the clinic, which had in its immunology department the facilities and physicians to handle unusual cases.

The negative report came during one of Jared's well periods, making it even harder to accept. But a few days later he had a serious relapse. We had friends visiting, and Jared had gone outside to play with their children. Marlene remembers being so proud of Jared that day, watching him run and play ball and ride his training bike with the other youngsters. That night his temperature shot up to 105 degrees for a few hours. Soon he was weak and delirious. Now we wanted to go back to the Mayo Clinic, but we were afraid Jared wouldn't survive another road trip.

Instead, we went back to the local allergy clinic that had recommended Jared's desensitizing shots. We didn't know it then, but our decision precipitated a new nightmare that is still with us. Seeing Jared's deteriorated mental and physical condition, the allergist now diagnosed him as mentally retarded and autistic. "His symptoms are eighty percent autism and twenty percent severe allergies. Because of the autism, he can't take any stress, even going outside, without falling apart. His symptoms are triggered by sensory bombardment, like changes in atmospheric pressure and temperature. His hypersensitive autonomic nervous system simply can't handle those changes."

She went on to say that, though Jared had allergies, his unusually severe symptoms could be explained, she felt, only by autism. In other words, he was overreacting to normal allergic symptoms. She didn't make it clear if she believed that retardation was caused by the autism or that both conditions had emerged simultaneously. I felt she was saying Jared was developmentally retarded because of the autism.

We were shocked by her diagnosis. Jared was trying so hard to function despite his great pain. He had always been extremely affectionate and never exhibited the strange behavioral patterns of autism, such as withdrawal, insistence on sameness, rocking and spinning. In fact, Jared now was too sick to even exhibit such behavior.

We didn't really believe the allergist's diagnosis, and we certainly weren't going to give up on Jared. The autism diagnosis seemed to be pulled from thin air. The allergist seemed to us to be groping for any diagnosis, based on nothing more than Jared's deafness and inability to speak. For the next twelve months, we traveled from one specialist to another, seeking another explanation. One pediatrician examined Jared and told us he was "grossly abnormal." Without asking about his medical history, he prescribed an antihistamine for Jared's congestion. When we described Jared's severe reaction to the drug, he blamed it on autism. We left his office angry and in tears.

Jared sank deeper into his illness. He couldn't

speak a word. His face was swollen and distorted. His coordination was so poor, he was back to crawling, except on the days he couldn't even crawl and would have to slide on his stomach to get to the bathroom.

As horrible as it seems, by this time our family so accepted the sick Jared that we never considered how deathly ill he must have looked to strangers. Then, one afternoon, Marlene called a repairman to fix the washing machine.

The man who came was a middle-aged Asian, and when he saw three-year-old Jared, swollen-faced, sliding across the floor on his stomach, the man sucked in his breath. "What's wrong with your son?"

"He has severe allergies," Marlene answered.

"Is he going to live?" The man twisted his face in a pained expression.

"I hope so."

"I'm sorry. I can't stay here. If your son dies while I'm here, I don't know what I would do—it's so sad." And he left.

Marlene closed the door, tears streaming down her face. It was an emotional moment, shared with a total stranger. She cried and cried.

We went to another pediatrician. This time the terrifying diagnosis was cystic fibrosis. It's an inherited disease, he told us, that affects the exocrine glands—those that produce mucus, sweat, and saliva —and results in the improper functioning of many organs, including the lungs. He said it explained Jared's excessive mucus and steadily deteriorating condition. He referred us to a local physician who specialized in treating children with the disease.

But, when I called the specialist and related all Jared's symptoms, including the retardation diagnosis, he felt cystic fibrosis wasn't indicated. "It sounds like your son may have an unusual immunological disorder," he said and suggested we contact a former colleague of his in the immunology department at the Baylor College of Medicine in Houston. Both had cared for David, the Houston "bubble boy."

Now we had two doctors theorizing that Jared's problem might be immunological. Marlene and I briefly considered taking Jared to Baylor, but in the end decided against starting with a new clinic without first completing the Mayo examination and getting their final diagnosis. Our primary concern was getting Jared well enough so we could take him back there.

We tried a new allergist who had been strongly recommended by our original pediatrician. When shown Jared's chart indicating extreme allergies to most airborne substances, this allergist said the tests had to be invalid, that it was impossible for a three-year-old to have become so allergic, that it would take years to build up such sensitivity. He gave Jared another series of skin tests. When they came back negative, confirming his theory, he put Jared on a diet of pears, lamb, and rice. Jared stayed on the diet for three weeks. He lost weight and his symptoms continued. On our return visit the allergist saw Jared, sick as ever, and he changed his diagnosis to retardation. He referred us back to the original pediatrician.

We estimate that, by that time, we had seen more than two dozen local doctors. Fortunately, our medical insurance covered most of the cost of the doctors' examinations and lab tests. But none of the doctors and none of their tests could help Jared. Most told us nothing more could be done for him. He was hopelessly retarded. When we protested that he had been completely normal for his first eighteen months and since had had periods of being strong and active, they didn't believe us. We knew the doctors were making the diagnosis because Jared was sick and so unresponsive that, to them, he looked truly retarded. Even if they did honestly think he was retarded, it was no consolation to us.

None of these doctors took Jared's developmental history. It seemed to us that they were using both "retarded" and "autistic" to describe Jared because they couldn't tell which was accurate just by looking at him. Presumably they felt that further tests by other experts would determine the final diagnosis.

It is often difficult just by a quick examination to distinguish between the two. Autism, a form of childhood schizophrenia, results in complete withdrawal from the world and usually includes lack of speech. Although not retarded in the strict medical sense, the autistic child functions at the level of a retarded child. But, unlike the truly retarded, some autistic children have been known to recover from their affliction and develop normally.

A truly retarded child, on the other hand, has only so much potential and never reaches a normal level of intelligence. Rather than withdrawing like the autistic child, the retarded child communicates at the level of his development. The autism diagnosis for Jared seems to have come simply from his inability to hear and communicate. A few pediatricians did say Jared might not be autistic, but deaf and retarded. At least one pediatrician and several ear doctors mentioned the difficulty of distinguishing among deafness, autism, and retardation in young children.

These were no more than casual comments and ideas thrown out to us. In reality the "referral system," which is supposed to ensure continuity of medical care, was now working against us. Typically, we would take Jared to a new doctor who would observe his failing condition, examine him, and then inquire about previous diagnoses and treatments. Told of the retardation diagnosis, the new doctor would come up with the same diagnosis and refer us to a center that places severely retarded children in institutions. The visits never lasted more than twenty minutes. No doctor proposed further medical treatment.

It was like going through a revolving door. Marlene and I would bring Jared home after each visit, exhausted by the futility of it, cry, and try to reassure each other that someday this terrible thing would be over. We still had reason to hope. While we saw Jared every day, the doctors saw him only when he was very sick. We knew what he was capable of, what he was like when he was free of his symptoms.

I guess you could say I learned about perseverance and never giving up from my father. As a child, growing up in New York, I remember my father, a successful clothing manufacturer, telling me never to give up, not to be a quitter. He'd tell me stories about how he'd almost failed in business several times, about how he'd hung on until finally the tide would turn and he would win. "Success might be only a few days away," he'd say. I carried these words with me through my college years and into my married life. Many times I would look at Jared and think, if Dad were here, he'd tell me not to give up.

Although we always knew we would never give up on Jared, we never had any special game plan to help him. We did whatever was necessary, whatever we felt was right. We always worked hard, confronting events as they evolved, always talking things through. Marlene and I work well together. A sick child would never break up our marriage. Jared's illness only drew us closer. During Jared's sick periods, we'd talk and talk late into the night. We'd spend hundreds of hours planning, speculating, forming hypotheses, rejecting hypotheses, before we'd finally decide what to do. Often we'd bounce these ideas off Marlene's parents, to get their opinion. I missed not being able to confide in my own parents.

We recall one such marathon discussion we had with Marlene's parents about Jared's deafness and inability to speak. Of course, they were shocked when they first heard about the autism diagnosis and our fears that he might never talk. Marlene and I had been discussing his condition for days, trying to find a way to prove to ourselves that Jared didn't talk because he was deaf. It was Marlene's mother who gave us that proof.

She led us into Jared's room and stood behind his crib, where he was lying awake. He hadn't seen us come in. Marlene's mother talked to him in a loud voice. No response. Then she moved to Jared's side so he could catch sight of her, and immediately Jared turned his head, smiled, and reached out for her to pick him up. Through tears, Marlene's mother picked him up, hugged and kissed him. "See," she said, "I told you he's deaf."

Over the next few weeks, we repeated the experiment. We would bang pots together, activate the smoke alarm, talk loudly—all behind his back—and Jared wouldn't move his head or respond. But the minute we were in his sight, he'd look at us and reach out to be picked up. We were convinced his deafness accounted for his unresponsiveness. But why?

Marlene had majored in physiology and psychology in college and, as part of her postgraduate work, had taken courses in immunology, virology, radiology, and pharmacology at a medical school. Now she started poring over medical books in the library. We spent hundreds of dollars buying every book we could find on allergies, retardation, and autism, but Jared's illness never fit any of the patterns described in the textbooks.

None of the allergy books reported cases as severe as Jared's, and the standard treatments and reliefs had actually intensified his symptoms. As for the autism diagnosis, Jared never showed any of the behaviors associated with the condition, nor did he look "exceptionally beautiful," as many of the books described autistic children. He didn't even look normal, but rather like a flawed doll. We conceded that, when ill, Jared did function at the level of a severely retarded child. But nowhere in the literature was mental retardation described as an on-again, off-again condition. Brain damage is permanent. He either had it, or he didn't.

We kept reading books and medical journals. It was Marlene who came across an article by a University of Oregon ear specialist who had devised a new way to insert tubes in the ears with a local anesthetic and without using antihistamines. We knew something had to be done about the fluid in Jared's ears, or he would become permanently deaf. When I phoned the doctor, he explained that the procedure wasn't done on children under six. But he did offer another solution to Jared's problem—air filters.

He said he had used filters successfully with his own three children, all of whom had suffered from severe allergies and ear fluid problems. The filters attach to the house's air-conditioning and heating system, removing pollen and dust from the air. It seemed like a sound scientific approach to me, the ultimate method of controlling allergies, avoiding the allergens altogether.

I decided to go ahead and track down a filtering system, and my research soon uncovered a 600-dollar system that removed 94 percent of the particles in the air.

"You don't treat retardation with a filter," one allergist said when I asked him if it was worth installing. I called another allergist and asked him if he thought the filters would work. His exasperation was intimidating: "The only way to avoid the allergens on earth is to go to the moon." I didn't buy the system.

Our original pediatrician tried a more potent drug, a cortisone inhalant he felt would help overcome Jared's inflammation. Jared took it for a few days, and it produced severe side effects that only intensified when he was taken off the drug. For three weeks Jared lay unresponsive in his crib—he was back in diapers and being fed from a baby bottle.

This was the lowest point in our struggle to save Jared. For the first time we really feared he had been permanently brain-damaged and wouldn't recover. Was it fair to let him suffer, we wondered. One doctor suggested we authorize ear surgery, which we could legally do, and so solve Jared's problem. The anesthesia and drugs he would have to take during surgery would be a form of euthanasia. "You should face the facts," the doctor said. "Jared wasn't meant to live in the first place."

We were almost ready to give in. We called Marlene's parents. Her mother, who was born during the Russian Revolution and had survived Stalin's pogroms, was no stranger to crisis and suffering. Her first concern was Jared.

"Is it really fair to Jared to let him suffer any more?" she asked us.

"I can't bear to see him die," Marlene said, almost choking on the words.

"Marlene, stop thinking of yourself! Start thinking of Jared. Your father and I are thinking of Jared now. He's the one who's living and suffering in constant pain."

Marlene got up and ran to Jared's room, sobbing. I found her there, stroking his arm gently.

"God, it's so good to be able to touch him. I'd never be able to touch him or feel his soft skin again."

"I feel the same way," I said. I held her tightly.

When I thought of buying a little coffin and burying Jared, I realized we weren't prepared to face death's finality. Our boy was still alive, and we could love him every day. Perhaps he would cheat death.

We talked with Marlene's parents late into the night. Our decision in the end was unanimous: Jared must live. It was the only decision we could really consider. We had a moral responsibility to direct his fate, to respect the value of this single life.

Right before Jared's fourth birthday, Marlene took him back to our pediatrician. Jared couldn't walk and just lay there on the examining table. "Please, please help us," Marlene begged the doctor.

He tried to give Jared an IQ test, but the only response he could elicit was from a tickle. "Be reasonable," he told Marlene. "You're the parent of a retarded and autistic child, and you have to accept it. You saw the IQ test, didn't you? That's it. There's simply no more anyone can do for Jared. I don't want to see him again, and from what I hear, neither does anyone else."

I was in the middle of a business conference when Marlene called. "I've just been to the pediatrician," she said between sobs. I could barely understand her. "Now he's saying Jared's retarded and autistic, and he doesn't want to see him anymore. We've run out of doctors!"

I remember saying, "What do you mean? What do you mean?" three or four times—it wouldn't sink in. I left work at once, sick with fear, hardly able to understand what was happening.

As soon as I walked in the door, I called the pediatrician and scheduled a meeting. This would be the first of a series of consultations we had that went on for four weeks. At the final meeting, Marlene asked him how he could give up on Jared, knowing he had been born a healthy and normal baby. I reminded him of times when Jared had played happily in his office. At last, and reluctantly, he told us the basis of his diagnosis—Jared was suffering from a degenerative disease that was destroying his brain. The illness, he felt, was similar to Tay-Sachs disease, an inherited, metabolic disorder that leads to retardation and early death.

"What about the times when Jared was well, not so long ago, when he was running and playing like a normal kid?" I asked. He didn't respond. Marlene was angry and crying now. "How can Jared be permanently brain-damaged? Just a few months ago he was whizzing down the sidewalk on his tricycle."

"You don't expect me to believe that, do you?" he asked.

"Call some of our friends! Ask them what Jared was like when he was well."

He ignored my suggestion. "Please don't be insulted, but I want you and your wife to consider seeing a psychiatrist, so you can learn to accept what's happened to Jared. You have to stop blaming yourselves for this."

We kept pleading with him not to give up on Jared. A month before, we'd phoned Stanford University Medical Center and asked to have Jared admitted for observation. We were told it was impossible without a referral, so now we begged the pediatrician to give us a referral to Stanford. He refused. Instead, he wrote out a referral to the state regional center to have Jared placed in a facility. The "facility," he said, would be a "humane place for Jared to spend his last days."

"No, we're not going to abandon Jared," we insisted.

He warned us not to fight his diagnosis. "It's almost impossible to fight a medical diagnosis. You'd have to go to court to change it, and as far as I know, parents have won in only one such case in California." The horror of what he was saying struck me like a physical blow. I could see what was coming, and it made me reel.

Driving home we were paralyzed, weak with despair. Marlene carried Jared into the house. He was so thin and pale, his body and face twisted in pain. He didn't know he had just been sentenced to die.

4

"I Love You, World!"

Jared began to recover, but again his recovery was short-lived. One morning he went outdoors to get a toy and passed out. He turned blue, and his body, his tongue, and his eyelids swelled grotesquely. Black-and-blue marks appeared all over his body, as they had before.

Marlene was home alone when it happened. Terrified, she gathered up four-year-old Jared and began to drive him to the hospital. She stopped after a few blocks. The doctors, she knew, might give him medications that could kill him. But if she kept him home, and he died, she might be accused of murder. Jared looked like he had been hit by a car. How could she explain to the doctors that a whiff of air had done this to him? They would think she had beaten him up.

Weeping, Marlene drove home, left Jared in the car, dashed into the house, and started to call me at work. Then she remembered I was out of town for the day. She ran back to the car and started driving around aimlessly. Jared had to be taken somewhere, she knew, but where? At a red light, she turned around to look at Jared stretched out on the back seat, motionless, swollen, black-and-blue.

Near hysterics, she kept driving. "Please, God," she prayed, "there has to be someone out there to help me!" Suddenly she realized she was lost, all alone on a two-lane country road, surrounded by unfamiliar rolling hills, pastures, farmhouses. Pickup trucks went by in slow motion. She began to wonder if she'd been transported to another time and place that was peaceful and somehow comforting. She just sat there for a while, then drove slowly through the eerie, twilight-zone landscape.

Two hours passed, Marlene was jolted back to reality by a road sign that read "Sacramento." An hour later she was home. She carried Jared to his bed.

When I came home from work, I couldn't comprehend the horror of what I saw. I tried to pick up Jared to take him to the doctor, but Marlene stopped me. "You can't, you can't," she said over and over. I stood there, holding Jared in my arms, listening to

Marlene's pleadings, until the helplessness of the situation hit me. We really couldn't take him to any local doctor or hospital. We had no one to turn to.

I gently laid him in his bed. For the next forty-eight hours, he kept slipping in and out of a coma. He was near death, and there was nothing we could do but sit by his side and pray he would live. Miraculously, he pulled through.

Somehow, this last crisis forced us to begin piecing together all the clues of the last three years. Only this emerged—the air outdoors made Jared worse. His infrequent good spells during the hot summer months when he stayed inside our air-conditioned house, his relief in shopping centers and air-conditioned restaurants, the setbacks as soon as he went outside, all confirmed our theory. In desperation, we decided to go ahead and try the air-filtering system.

The first unit we tried was a portable electrostatic unit we put in Jared's room. It gave off an unpleasant ozone odor, so I returned it the next day and kept looking. One of the contractors I called recommended a high-efficiency air-cleaning unit that attached to the central heating and cooling system we had in our house. It could trap a wide range of particles—pollen, mold spores, feathers, pet dander, hair, dust—as small as .01 microns (a micron is 1/25,000 of an inch). The system could filter out 99 percent of ragweed pollen, for example. I ordered the unit.

The night it hummed into operation, Jared went to bed with his usual wheezing and cries of pain. I left for work in the morning, and Marlene sat waiting for Jared to announce his waking, as he always did now, by crying. At ten o'clock, she phoned me. She couldn't hear Jared's usual labored breathing, and he never slept more than five hours at a time. It was fifteen hours since he had gone to bed.

"Barry, please come home. I think something's happened to Jared. I can't hear him breathing."

"Go open his door and check him," I said, trying to reassure her that everything probably was all right.

"I can't do it myself. Please, come home!"

"Maybe he's just sleeping."

"No, he never sleeps this long. Something's happened."

"You'll have to check him, Marlene. Come on. Pull the extension phone over to his room, then open the door. I'll be right here."

I hung on. The suspense was tearing me apart. Then I heard Marlene laughing, crying out, "Jared! Jared!" She'd found our four-year-old boy sitting up in bed, smiling, breathing evenly, the flow of mucus from his nose gone.

"I can't believe it—he's well, Barry."

"It's the filters. My God, they worked. I had a feeling they'd work."

"I don't know, it's just so fast, like a miracle. He looks like he's healed."

It *was* a miracle. The filters worked, and they kept on working.

Over the next two weeks, Jared's symptoms disappeared one by one. He was a little boy again, free of pain, attacking life with zest. He slept long and peacefully. His appetite returned, and so did his hearing.

I felt like a new dad again. When I'd come home at night, Jared would greet me at the front door. He'd run toward me with outstretched arms and a big smile. Picking him up and holding his warm little body in my arms, I'd hug and kiss him—and give thanks to God that he was alive and well. Jared had returned to the world. Our sleepless nights were past. We could function like a normal family again. Like a blind man who'd been given sight, I knew I'd appreciate every minute I could spend with Jared. I would never waste it or take it for granted. I knew what it meant.

As Jared emerged from his silent world, he heard ordinary household sounds like the dishwasher, telephone, and television, for the first time and was frightened by them. He had taken showers since he was very little, but one night he apparently heard the water running for the first time in his memory. He stumbled terrified out of the bathroom. After calming him, we introduced him to the sound of running water in the kitchen faucet, first a dribble, then full force. He came to love the sound of splashing water and all the other new and strange sounds around him. He would press his ear against every appliance in the house, listening, squealing with delight.

Now that Jared could hear, Marlene's days were filled with a joyful new project—teaching him to talk. She did it under the direction of the John Tracy Clinic for deaf and hard-of-hearing children. Months earlier we'd enrolled Jared in a correspondence course at the clinic and began what turned out to be a very rewarding association with the clinic's correspondence teacher. We'd given her background on Jared's problems, our frustrating encounters with doctors, our ineffectual efforts to help him.

Each month, the teacher sent us a lesson and an encouraging letter and, indeed, became our greatest source of help and comfort during that difficult time. Now this wonderful woman shared our joy in having found a way to "save" Jared. She wrote that she was quite familiar with the effect allergies and middle-ear problems have on young children's language development, and that she was very excited by our success with the air-filtering system. "The whole field of biomedical engineering in developing new equipment has always intrigued me," she wrote. "I think we'll see exciting progress in this field, possibly for our deaf children, certainly for the blind."

Marlene began teaching Jared to talk by sitting close to him, speaking directly into his ear, and letting him touch her mouth so he could hear her voice's vibrations. It was a wonderful and emotional moment for all of us when, six weeks later, he suddenly realized that sound came from her mouth. He touched her lips, over and over, silently asking her to talk. Using his sense of touch, he gradually learned what objects made "sound."

For hours every day, Marlene poured as much language as she could into Jared, trying to get him to understand conversation and to speak. Jared would sit opposite her, looking directly at her face as she spoke. He learned to lip-read in this way and absorbed language so quickly that soon he could comprehend ordinary conversational speech just like any child his age.

Unfortunately, his intelligence and spirit worked against our efforts to get him to speak. Over the years of his illness, he had developed a sophisticated gesture language that got him everything he needed. He looked like he was acting out a fast-moving game of charades, with intricate hand and body movements. When his grandmother visited, he'd greet her and motion for her to sit down by crossing his legs and bending down into a half-squatting position. He developed an uncanny sense of direction, too, and knew every road we'd traveled by car. By pointing, he effortlessly directed us from home all the way to the toy store, restaurants, his grandmother's house, or the park.

Now, though he could hear and understand us, he felt no need to speak. He kept gesturing and wouldn't say a word. If we asked him a question, he would shake his head or nod. If he wanted something, he'd imitate the activity or point to it. He seemed to have forgotten that he ever had talked.

Marlene tried to take advantage of Jared's interest in books—he would point to the words and gesture for her to say them aloud. She made sandpaper alphabet cards and taught Jared to trace them with his fingers, while she made the letter sounds. Because of his highly developed sense of touch, Jared learned to distinguish the letters easily, and as Marlene would say a letter, he would point to the correct one. But he still wouldn't utter a sound.

I really considered Marlene Jared's teacher, so I didn't help with the speech therapy. Instead, I made up for lost time with nine-year-old David. Evenings and weekends we'd work together building model rockets propelled by solid fuel that we'd launch in an open area. David's favorite was a three-foot scale model of a German V-2 rocket. After countdown and ignition, he'd stand back and proudly watch his rocket zoom up to 700 feet and gently parachute back to earth. It was an impressive sight and always attracted a crowd.

We got crowds, too, when we launched a nine-foot-high, red-and-white-striped, hot-air balloon David built. He also built a rocket and installed an aerial camera that worked beautifully, automatically taking color shots of the landscape from an altitude of 1,000 feet. David's skills and ingenuity thrilled me. My pride was only matched by David's, when he showed his pictures of "Earth" to his school friends.

One-year-old Alicia was a very good baby, not demanding at all. She was healthy and was developing normally. This was a good break for Marlene, because Jared needed so much of her time. Alicia, truly patient, waited until we had time for her, usually in the evenings when Jared was in his room. During the day, when Marlene was working with Jared, Alicia would play contentedly at their feet. As long as she was near Marlene and Jared, she was satisfied.

In the meantime, Marlene was wonderfully persistent with Jared. She made twenty cards, on which she wrote commands such as walk, stand up, lie down, run, jump. Introducing one card at a time, she'd say the word on the card and have Jared act it out. Once he had learned to read all the cards, Marlene would simply hold up a card, silently, and Jared would carry out the command energetically. Next

Marlene introduced him to simple nouns and verbs on cards. Again, Jared learned all the words in short order and soon could arrange them into short sentences, a "game" that delighted him more than anything. Within a few weeks, he was using the cards to communicate with us. Still, there were no words from him. We sensed we'd have to do something quickly, or he might remain silent forever.

I phoned a speech therapist, and we had a long discussion about Jared. "You may have to force him to talk," she told me. "Stop responding to his gestures, and let's see what happens." Marlene started immediately playing dumb to Jared's gestures. When he motioned for something, she would act attentive but confused. "What did you say?" she'd ask him. He grew more and more angry and finally started throwing temper tantrums. He would fling himself to the floor, kicking and screaming until he was exhausted.

Finally Jared's need to communicate became so urgent, he had hourly outbursts, and his gestures became wild and emphatic. The struggle got more physical. For several weeks, every time Jared gestured for something, Marlene put her hands on his shoulders and firmly pushed him down to a sitting position. "If you want something, you'll have to ask for it!"

One evening, as Marlene was putting Jared to bed, he looked up at her and said, "Go to bed." He had broken the language barrier. It shocked him so much, he crumpled against Marlene and cried from happiness. "Barry, come into Jared's room! He talked!" she shouted to me. We laughed and sobbed at the same time, hugging and kissing him.

After that evening, Jared talked more and more every day. He went from single words to full sentences in a few months. When he started to talk, his biggest joy was giving commands: "Get milk... make pancakes... call Grandma." We were so delighted to hear him talk, I'm afraid we gave into his every demand. At first his speech, awkward and slurred, sounded like that of a deaf child, but his articulation improved with time and practice.

Now that he could talk and hear, Jared's curiosity was never satisfied. Marlene spent six hours a day with him, teaching him all the things he had missed during his sick years. It became a breathless race for her to keep up with him, his mind was working so rapidly. They pored over picture books. Jared especially liked outrageously silly stories like Dr. Seuss's and books with information about the natural world. He loved reading about how things work, and he and Marlene did simple scientific experiments together. He kept an ant farm and a large collection of rocks and leaves in his room. He captured every little creature that invaded his room and put it in his bug collector. Marlene bought educational materials from a school supply store, and from these Jared learned about the globe, human anatomy, and plant development. With blocks and number rods, he learned to count and add and subtract. Solving math problems became a favorite activity, and he loved using first- and second-grade arithmetic books. We watched Jared fill his days with wonder and learning, and we almost couldn't believe this was the same boy who a few months before was near death.

Jared and David now became close friends. They spent every evening playing cops and robbers and competitive board games, making up for the years they had lost. Though opposite in personality—David was sensitive, independent, and serious, while Jared was quick-moving, energetic, intense, and volatile—they got along remarkably well. While they played, little Alicia would sit nearby watching, often trying to join in by tumbling board pieces or otherwise messing up their games. The boys loved her so much, they tolerated her intrusions gladly.

Jared was filled with excess energy, so I began making weekly trips to buy toys to keep him occupied. Mechanical toys were his favorite, Erector Set, Rivitron Construction Set, Nuts and Bolts, Lego, Mechano. He would sit totally absorbed and animated, building elaborate pulleys, skyscrapers, and bridges. Then he discovered my tool chest and quickly learned to use the screwdriver, hammer, pliers, and wrench. His mechanical ability, which was just developing when he first got sick, now seemed uncanny. He managed to take apart and reassemble beds, tables, faucets, and the radio intercom. Finally he began unhinging doors and cupboards and, with mischievous delight, watched each one fall when I went to open it.

After six months in the house, even his mechanical pastimes started to bore him. He would stand at the window, watching other children play, with longing. "Why don't they get sick outside?" he'd ask us. "Will they get sick tonight?" He tried to venture outside once, but his old affliction returned instantly. "That outside is a son of a bitch!" he shouted, as he ran back into the house. He refused to go outside again.

We were surprised and disappointed at the

speed and intensity of the symptoms that day. Jared had been virtually free of his illness for half a year, and even colds and the flu hadn't caused any setbacks. We knew we'd have to find a way to get him out into the world safely soon. In a few months, he'd be old enough to start kindergarten. He needed to play outside with children his own age, go to the park and the zoo, take vacations.

During a heavy rainstorm one night, Jared disappeared from his room. The noise of the storm had awakened me, and I did a quick check of the children's windows. Jared wasn't in his bed or anywhere in the house. Marlene and I searched frantically. The front door was open. Then the thought hit me: Jared must have awakened during the storm and probably sensed the heavy rains had cleansed the air. Instinctively, I went to the park, a block away. There was Jared, running about, rolling in the grass, hugging and kissing the trees, and shouting, "I love you, world!"

5 *One Small Step—*
Outside—
for Jared

Four-year-old Jared now had one thing on his mind —getting outside. In the mornings, Marlene would find him standing in his room with his face pressed against the window, staring longingly outside.

"Can I go out and play?" he'd ask Marlene.

"Sure, if you'd like to, go on," she would answer, knowing that if he sensed conditions were right, as he had the night it rained, he'd go out on his own.

"No, I can't go out. I get sick out there." And that was how it ended each morning.

Weeks passed, and Jared became more and more unhappy with his confinement. He lost interest in his toys. He'd build with his blocks for a while, then kick them down in frustration. Because he had nothing worthwhile to do after eating, he'd take as much time as he could at the table, shoving food around his plate, eating slowly, taking seconds and thirds. Mealtimes became long, drawn-out affairs. The house was a prison to him. We knew we had to get him out.

Our first idea was to contact his local doctors, hoping Jared's recovery would encourage them to explore his symptoms once again and maybe come up with a treatment or cure. I came home early from work one afternoon to phone his pediatrician. Expecting to have a long conversation with him as in the past, I settled myself comfortably and began dialing the number, all the time imagining how pleased the doctor would be when I told him Jared was well and walking and talking. But the receptionist said the doctor wasn't in. I was so geared up to give the good news, I blurted out my story about Jared's recovery to her. She could hear him laughing and talking in the background.

"Is that him I hear?" she asked, excited.

"Yes, that's him."

"God! That's a real miracle. I can't wait to tell the doctor."

I told her to give the doctor the message that he was welcome to visit us at home and see Jared for himself. She thought that was a wonderful idea. "You'll be hearing from the doctor soon, I'm sure."

For three days, every time the phone rang, Marlene and I would jump up, thinking it was the doctor, but it never was. To make sure he knew I had called, I called again and left a brief message, this time with a different receptionist. The doctor never responded.

It seemed we'd been abandoned by the pediatrician. How could a doctor not care that a patient who once was dying now was well? I will never forget his words at our last visit—that we couldn't change a medical diagnosis except through a court case. We always thought he'd said that because he truly believed Jared was irreversibly retarded.

Now we wondered if he really meant he wouldn't change his diagnosis, no matter what. I also remembered him saying at that final visit that he didn't want to see Jared anymore, and from what he'd heard neither did any other local doctors. I decided not to try to contact any more doctors. If the one who knew us so well could be so callous, I figured the others might be, too. Emotionally, I was spent. I couldn't take any more letdowns.

Years later I discovered my pessimism had been well-founded. In 1982 I picked up a copy of the Lanterman Developmental Disabilities Services Act at the state health and welfare agency. Section 4656(b) of the act states that "each regional center shall maintain a record of every developmentally disabled person under the age of eighteen years known by the regional center to have been referred to it for its services, whether or not services are actually provided." My original guess probably had been right. Once the retardation diagnosis was in the state records, other doctors became aware of it and wouldn't go against a fellow doctor to change it.

But Jared had to get outside, and quickly. The only other thing I could think of was portable filtering equipment he could wear outside. To find it, if it existed, would be a mammoth research job. I took a week off from work and started by phoning the respiratory therapy sections of a dozen prominent hospitals scattered around the country and asking for advice. Most said they were aware of the need for such equipment, but they didn't know if it was available. One hospital staff member said they were planning to start research on such a project within a year. He offered to keep me informed. I called the American Lung Association and several biomedical engineering laboratories with no success. Portable filtering systems designed especially for allergy sufferers apparently didn't exist.

I finally decided to look into equipment used to protect workers in polluted areas, hoping that their equipment might also filter out allergens. My first encouraging lead came from an engineer at the Kaiser Aluminum and Chemical Corporation in Oakland, California. He said a device that would be adaptable to a child did, indeed, exist in the health and safety field. He suggested I try an adjustable, battery-powered respirator made by an East Coast safety equipment manufacturer.

My call to the manufacturer paid off. After I explained Jared's problem, the sales manager offered to send us free of charge one of their portable respirators, which blew filtered air into a plastic helmet. I literally ran from the phone to tell Marlene the news.

It was a beautifully designed piece of equipment —but it didn't fit Jared. It was too heavy and bulky for a four-year-old. However, it did fit David perfectly, so we weren't completely disappointed. Eventually Jared would be able to wear ready-made equipment, and the fact that it existed at all encouraged us. I started looking for a respirator that would fit Jared.

Over the next few weeks, I phoned many manufacturers, but none made a portable unit small enough for a little boy. I began toying with the idea of devising a filtering mask on my own and started by researching filtering materials that would work. My first call was to the Lawrence Livermore National Laboratory, where I reached Bruce Held, an industrial hygienist and an expert on air filters. That he was the person I was referred to when I called that day still feels like luck, even after all these years.

I started to tell him what I was trying to make, but, halfway through, he interrupted me. "Would you like me to build your son a portable, battery-powered air purifier?" Tears came as I sat at my desk at work, and I choked out, "Yes, yes. Thank you."

Three weeks later I got an excited call from Held. "Barry, the helmet is finished. You can pick it up anytime. Jared's really going to like the headgear. It looks just like an astronaut's helmet." In fact, he said, it had become a popular item among the neighborhood children who were around when his own little daughter, about the same size as Jared, had modeled it for him.

I went to pick up the new equipment at Held's home that Friday after work. Held, tall and dignified, met me at the door, then led me into his study, which was lined with many plaques and public service awards. My benefactor was a recognized humanitarian.

When Held brought out the equipment, I was impressed immediately by how compact and light it was. He explained about the blower motor, which pulls in outside air through high-efficiency air filters and pumps it through a hose to the helmet; that the unit was designed so pressure inside the helmet is always higher than outside, to prevent dirty air from leaking in; and how the unit can run for four hours on a battery pack that can be recharged overnight. The motorized portion weighed only about five pounds and could fit easily into a small backpack. The blue lightweight-plastic helmet, with a clear plastic visor, had a soft fabric hood suspended from the helmet that could be tied with a drawstring at the neck. This small marvel would provide Jared with 99.97 percent purified air.

As Held finished explaining the unit and its maintenance, I tried to find intelligent words to thank him. All I could say, though, was, "Thank you. Thank you," over and over.

"All the thanks I want is the satisfaction that I helped your son. Just be sure to let me know how it's working out."

Marlene ran out to meet me in the garage when I got home. I opened the car trunk. She looked down at the helmet, worried. "What if it doesn't work? I don't know if I could take it. Everything—Jared's future, our future—depends on it."

"Okay, let's wait awhile before we try it." I closed the trunk.

Marlene and I were so apprehensive about the helmet, so tense, we hardly spoke to each other all weekend. We were in a daze.

It was three days before we finally worked up the courage to try it out. I called Jared into the living room, showed him the helmet and backpack, turned on the blower and let him feel the stream of air that was flowing into the helmet.

"Would you like to try it on and go outside?"

"No, I don't like the helmet," he said quickly.

"Why?"

"The noise scares me!"

To ease Jared's fears, I asked David to put on the equipment and show Jared how much fun it was to wear. David jumped at the chance and, pretending he was an invader from outer space, started chasing a delighted Jared around the room. It wasn't long before Jared's instinct to play overrode his fear. He put on the helmet and backpack, and both boys continued the chase.

"Jared, why don't you go outside and play space invaders?" I asked him casually.

"No. I get sick out there."

"Look, you'll feel good outside if you wear this special helmet. It was made just for you so you *can* go outside."

He relented. "Okay, Daddy." He walked slowly to the front door. David ran ahead of him, urging him on. Then, looking like an astronaut who had just fallen from the face of the moon, Jared cautiously stepped out.

"Come on, come on!" David shouted.

Jared took another step out.

David cried, "One small step for Jared, one big step for this family!"

David took Jared's hand and led him into the front yard. He wandered about, picked some nectarines off the tree, then climbed up the large pear tree with David. There they sat on a low branch, surveying the surroundings, grinning.

Half an hour later, we brought Jared inside. Helmet off, his eyes sparkling and his cheeks glowing, he drew Marlene and me near him and hugged and kissed us. "I love my space helmet."

We loved it too. It was a miraculous breakthrough, providing even cleaner air than the house filters. We gradually extended Jared's time outside to the full four-hour battery time. Every day he would ask Marlene to put on his helmet so he could go out and play. And every day was a new thrill for him. He and David would ride their bikes in the yard or on the patio, or they'd give Alicia rides in the red wagon. On hot days, David would fill the wading pool, where all three would play with their water toys.

Four-year-old Jared wanted badly to be like the other children in the neighborhood, and soon he asked for his first bicycle. The two-wheeled, gold-colored trainer bike we bought quickly became his old, trusted friend. When he had his bike with him at the playground, he knew that other children would come over to play with him.

Actually, the children didn't need that inducement. They were fascinated by Jared's helmet, and many of them asked how they could get one of their own. It must have looked like the real thing. Once, a boy of about eleven was riding by on his bike and caught sight of Jared. He stopped suddenly, alarmed, jumped off his bike and ran away at top speed, fleeing for safety from the creature from outer space.

Outings that were commonplace to other youngsters were new and wonderful for Jared. At the zoo he stood fascinated, as all the animals from his picture books came alive. He would point and proudly name them: "Elephant, zebra, giraffe . . ." Shopping was another novel experience. Marlene would take Jared to buy clothes, and he'd bounce in and out of the dressing room, trying on every pair of jeans or shirt that he fancied.

He and Marlene had to go shopping often, for now that he played outside regularly, digging in the dirt, climbing trees, crawling under fences, he wore out his clothes fast. Looking at his dirty jeans at the end of the day was a happy reminder of how normal his life had become.

But time hadn't dimmed Jared's memory of his past pain. One morning, Marlene found him sitting on the sofa, his legs crossed, just laughing. When she asked what was so funny, he smiled broadly. "I just remembered, I used to be sick all the time."

Another morning, he came running into our bedroom, his eyes wild with fear. "Daddy, the filters aren't working. I'm getting sick." I jumped out of bed and checked the blower, but everything seemed all right. Then Jared's face started swelling, and he complained of a severe headache. I quickly called out a repairman, who found a worn belt slipping on the blower motor that supplies filtered air throughout the house. The filters were working at only 50 percent capacity. Once the belt was replaced, Jared recovered in a few hours. It was a grim reminder that his life still depended on the equipment.

Jared was now almost five years old and eligible to enter kindergarten. Though his outdoor equipment gave him great flexibility, it had two definite limitations that would have to be overcome for him to start school: a four-hour battery life and motor noise. Again Bruce Held stepped in to help. He contacted the manager of a large Midwestern manufacturing company who, on hearing about Jared's problem, offered to donate a larger-powered air purifier worth more than $800. It could be plugged into an ordinary electrical outlet or a car's cigarette lighter. At school, the motor could be placed outside the classroom and a long flexible hose run to the helmet, thus eliminating motor noise.

After the equipment arrived, the manager of the company's occupational health and safety division in the Midwest made a special trip to our home to instruct us in the equipment's proper use. He had spent the last two months coordinating with the company's legal department the release of the equipment to us. Our intended use was experimental—for medical purposes, instead of occupational safety—so we had to sign several release papers that company attorneys had drawn up. All the equipment parts were labeled "Experimental."

The manager assembled and demonstrated the unit in our car. It worked beautifully. The blower motor, plugged into the cigarette lighter and placed on the car floor, pumped filtered air through a hose to Jared's helmet. Operating time was virtually unlimited, and Jared was very comfortable since he didn't have to wear the backpack.

We spent two busy days with the manager, who shared our excitement about the unit's value for Jared. He told us the company was aware of the equipment's potential for thousands of people with allergies to airborne substances who aren't helped by medication or desensitization.

"You know," he said, "this equipment was introduced just a little while ago. The company's looking into the idea of developing it as a medical product, so we're really interested in following Jared's progress."

We were gratified that this advanced technology had become available in time to give Jared a better life. When medicine couldn't help, private industry had stepped in. We were impressed that these people had done so much to help a little boy. Contrary to the popular idea of big business as profit-oriented and impersonal, we found the companies who helped us benevolent and people-oriented.

A colleague of mine at work, whom I had told about Jared's new equipment, urged me to contact a friend of his, the science editor of a local newspaper. This colleague knew something of Marlene's and my difficulties with Jared's medical problem, and he felt the story might benefit others with similar problems.

The editor was indeed interested and set up an appointment for the next week. When he and his photographer arrived, they were met by Jared, whizzing along the sidewalk, helmet bobbing, legs pumping his bicycle. The photographer pursued Jared at a fast clip and started snapping pictures. But

Jared increased his speed, gave the photographer a catch-me-if-you-can look, and finally jumped off his bike and darted into the house. Smiling happily and loving all the attention, he took off his gear. He talked with the photographer for a while, then led him to see his room and all his toys.

The photographer didn't know that nine short months before, Jared was near death, or that he had captured in pictures a Jared that no doctor believed had existed or could ever exist—strong, affectionate, bursting with life.

Marlene and I sat down in our living room with the editor and told him how the house filters and portable headgear had changed Jared's life. I explained Jared's symptoms and the unsuccessful efforts to treat him with medications and shots. I didn't mention the retardation diagnosis or that the doctors had given up on Jared or that they had recommended institutionalization. I just didn't want to embarrass the local doctors.

"Boy's life . . . Pure Delight" was the headline on the editor's story when it appeared on the front page of our local newspaper, complete with a photo of Jared riding his bike. The wire services, Associated Press and United Press International, picked up the story, and soon it was appearing worldwide. Calls started coming from reporters as far away as England and Germany. At first, because of our busy schedules, we turned down any other interviews, but the calls continued and soon included radio and television reporters. Finally we set aside two days for all the media.

Jared was feeling mischievous and rambunctious when the television crews arrived. He raced down the street on his bike and managed to elude the cameramen until one of them, wise to Jared's tricks, got into his van, opened his side sliding door, and as the van drove down the street, managed to capture the speeding Jared. "Someday we'll probably be covering him in the Olympics!" said the cameraman. Jared's metamorphosis was on video, a more or less permanent record for all to see.

We began to receive letters from people around the world who were facing problems similar to Jared's. They wanted to know all about his equipment, and many asked for the names of the physicians who had prescribed the outdoor equipment. We had to say we were sorry, but that the equipment was experimental and had been supplied by an industrial firm. The firm couldn't legally sell the equipment to allergy patients without government approval. All we could do was give them the name of our house filtering system, which was available commercially.

That Jared's equipment was desperately needed in the health field became more apparent when we started getting calls from doctors who wanted a similar unit for their patients. One caller was a pediatric surgeon at a hospital in Oakland, California, whose son had asthma, was housebound and badly needed the portable filter device. Medications had been ineffective, and the drug's side effects were so severe the boy couldn't function. The father said he envisioned the device connected to a tentlike canopy in the boy's bedroom, giving the child respite from his asthma attacks and enough relief so he could go outside for longer spells. The man's story pained us. We wanted to give him the name of the manufacturer who had supplied Jared's portable system, but we couldn't.

Doctors clearly were becoming more aware of the technology and its potential, and after all our searching for the equipment, the budding awareness pleased us. An allergy specialist from Denver wrote us: "I would like very much a follow-up on what . . . transpires with Jared over the long run and would be most interested in the details of the technology involved in the helmet. . . . We, of course, occasionally face the kind of problem you are describing, and it has been most frustrating trying to come up with a satisfactory apparatus. If you have something going here, I am sure there are a lot of other youngsters who might benefit from this information."

One year, to the day, after our last consultation with Jared's pediatrician, we received a copy of a French magazine. A three-page article on Jared carried a full-page picture of him hugging a little girl while they played in the park. Incredibly, a year before, we were almost ready to accept Jared's imminent death. We never would have believed it was possible that, in twelve months, Jared would recover totally, learn to speak and read, and become a normal boy; get equipment that would let him play, sleep, and, soon, go to school safely; and receive worldwide media coverage. At the time we thought the coverage was over, that the articles would become nothing more than a permanent memory of Jared's first happy days. We had no inkling of the critical role the press was yet to play in keeping Jared healthy and safe.

II   *The Dark Side of the Law*

6

Haunted by an Error

Jared turned five. The year was 1977, and the federal "mainstreaming" law, PL 94–142, had just been enacted. Called the Education of Handicapped Children Act, it guarantees all such children the right to a public school education. It mandates that each handicapped child be placed in the "least restrictive environment," to encourage his or her growth and development. Based on the premise that every child has potential, it calls on educators, parents, therapists, and other professionals to first evaluate the child's talents and limitations before choosing the best educational environment.

To Marlene and me, the new law assured that Jared could start kindergarten on time. I phoned the principal of our neighborhood public school, who scheduled a meeting for the following week to discuss, he said, mainstreaming Jared into the public school system. We had happy visions of Jared going off to school like other children, participating in classroom activities just like his peers.

I began the meeting in the principal's office by describing Jared's medical history and showing him the equipment that had been designed for school use. I hadn't been there more than ten minutes when the principal told me, quite abruptly, that he didn't think Jared could be successfully integrated into the school. "I'm going to give you a referral to another school that will be much more appropriate for Jared. They have a better staff and facilities to take care of him. I'll notify the school of the referral right away."

My distinct impression was that this other school would have smaller classes and more individualized attention, and the principal said nothing that suggested the impression wasn't true. Marlene and I talked about the meeting when I got home, and though we were disappointed that Jared wouldn't be going to the neighborhood school, we were pleased that soon he would be part of the public school system.

Nothing could have prepared us for the shock of what we were about to see at the "more appropriate" school. Marlene and I met with the school principal, who seemed anxious to have Jared as a student. The school, he said, had special trained teachers to deal with physically handicapped children, and Jared's equipment would be no trouble at all. Then he led us to the classrooms to meet the teachers and children.

Most of the children could neither walk nor talk. Many lay helplessly on mattresses. A few teenagers were being taught to walk by teachers' aides. Some children had brain shunts, tubes inserted in their brains to drain off fluid and so relieve pressure. We felt like invisible bystanders—the children never even noticed we were there.

In the rooms, spacious and beautifully decorated, we saw no evidence of any academic curriculum, no books, blackboards, desks. We had entered a world we didn't know existed. It seemed so unfair. Why did this have to happen to innocent youngsters? My mind flashed back to Jared a year before. If we hadn't found a way to save him, he would have joined the world of these children. Somehow, Jared had been dealt a different fate. He no longer was like them, and we felt almost guilty for being so blessed. But, clearly, the school was the end of mainstreaming for Jared.

We tried to piece together the reasons for Jared having been referred to a school for the handicapped. Why was he being denied the kind of education guaranteed under the new law? The principal of our neighborhood school, it seems, had never taken me seriously when I tried to enroll Jared as a normal student. That's why he gave us a referral without ever seeing Jared. We wondered if someone had contacted him before our meeting, to tell him our son had been diagnosed as retarded.

   We decided to try to challenge Jared's placement in the school for the handicapped by getting his IQ tested independently. We phoned several psychologists, but all of them wanted the name of our pediatrician, the diagnosis, and our reasons for wanting the test. When we described Jared's illness and told them of the retardation diagnosis, all refused to administer the test without first calling our pediatrician. One psychologist even told me that, as long as a child is doing well in school, no outside test was needed. I protested in vain about his "catch-22" reasoning. The retardation diagnosis prevented Jared from entering a regular public school, so there was no way to tell if he'd do well. On the other hand, no one would administer an IQ test, which might determine his ability to function in a regular school, so he could only be placed in a school for the handicapped —and there it was impossible for him to "do well." The psychologist couldn't deny my reasoning, but, he said, he still had to call the pediatrician.

   Our first concern was Jared's education. If we had decided to try to get the retardation diagnosis changed and keep Jared in the public school system, we would have had to go to court to fight it. We were in no financial position to wage a costly legal battle, and a court case could have delayed Jared's education until the case was resolved. Then, too, the delay might have given credence to the diagnosis, since Jared's lack of education would have resulted in lower test scores.

   We had another compelling reason for deciding against a legal fight—we couldn't risk Jared's life. In court, doctors might have asked that Jared's bubble be removed, so they could have another chance to treat him with medications, shots, or other therapy. We had good reason to suspect they might have tried this, since they believed Jared was retarded and didn't need his equipment. Because doctors are the experts in medical matters, our protests about removing Jared from his bubble might have fallen on deaf ears. We felt sure of one thing—we were so happy Jared was alive and well that we weren't going to do anything to jeopardize his life.

We felt the easiest way to fight back was to send him to a private school where he'd receive a normal education. If we wanted to go to court later on, we knew a good report card would be a powerful weapon against the retardation diagnosis. The medical experts would then be left in the position of having to explain to the court why a child who was doing well in school was, in fact, severely retarded and didn't belong in school!

David, then a fourth grader, was enrolled in a small private school for advanced students. It was a lovely place in a farmlike setting, with a large meadow and flowing brook. David had thrived physically and mentally in this rural and casual setting. We'd maintained a close relationship with the school's director, a warm and caring woman, during David's three years there. After hearing of Jared's needs and our problems with the public schools, she gladly accepted Jared without qualms.

Five-year-old Jared began attending kindergarten two hours a day, three days a week. Unfortunately, the school didn't have an electrical outlet outside the classroom for the noisy motor, nor any protected area adjacent to Jared's classroom where the equipment could be placed safely. So Jared couldn't use his large, plug-in unit. He was limited to his portable headgear. Despite his shortened school days, Jared played happily with his classmates, who accepted him without question. He also was a quick and eager student, and his teacher considered moving him ahead to first grade after seeing his good math and reading skills.

Jared had been in school only two weeks when the director called us, sounding extremely upset, and asked us to meet with her the next day. Since she didn't explain the problem, we spent an anxious twenty-four hours waiting for the meeting, sensing something was seriously wrong. It certainly wasn't Jared, who had come home from school that day well and happy as ever.

It turned out to be worse than anything we could have imagined in our worst nightmares. She told us that representatives from a governmental Social Services agency had visited the school the day before and demanded that the director hand over Jared to them for testing and placement in a facility for retarded children.

"I refused. I told them Jared wasn't retarded, but they were adamant and threatened to physically take him off the premises. I was shaking, but I managed to order them to leave." The Social Services officials started arguing, she told us, and threatened to return with the legal authorities to pick up Jared. "I'd never hand Jared over to them. They've tried this before with a few other students, and I didn't give in."

We listened in disbelief. Why would the state

want to interfere in our lives and take Jared away? We had worked for years to give him a normal life. He now was a lively child, free of his symptoms, flourishing in a sound academic environment. By attending a private school, he certainly was no financial burden to the state. If they got hold of him, they would place him with retarded children and his mental development would be stifled.

"Why do you think Social Services is doing this?" we asked the director. Her explanation was chilling. Under the law, once a child is diagnosed as retarded, the state is responsible for his or her care. In essence, the parents no longer control the child's destiny.

The law was enacted to protect retarded children, to ensure they get proper care and education and are not neglected by parents or teachers, so they can develop to their full potential. But, the director told us, there's a dark side to the law. "Whenever the state intervenes in your life, there's a chance for abuse. In Jared's case, they can use the law to perpetuate their retardation diagnosis. Through Social Services they can deny Jared a normal education, and if they do that, their diagnosis will become the prognosis."

It seemed clear to us that the doctors were trying to cover up their mistake. Without a normal education, Jared would, in effect, develop only to the level of a retarded child, and their diagnosis would become self-fulfilling. The law was on the doctors' side. So who would protect Jared from his protectors?

"With the law against us, what can we do?" we asked the director.

"There's just no simple solution. But I do know

of some other parents who've found themselves in a similar situation. I'm going to give you the name of the parents of a girl who was misdiagnosed as re-tarded. She's doing well in another private school. Maybe you'll learn something by talking to them." I talked with the girl's father that same day. He seemed eager to share their experiences and invited Marlene and me to talk with them at their house.

The parents introduced us to their eight-year-old daughter, a beautiful blond girl with a winning smile. This was the parents' story of their struggle to get a normal education for her.

She'd been born with a hearing impediment that delayed her language development. When they went to enroll her in a public school, she was placed in a class for mentally retarded children. The parents didn't fight the placement at first, though they knew their daughter was mentally alert. Soon it became obvious that she wasn't making any academic prog-ress, so the father went to the school officials and asked that she be placed in a normal class. After much haggling, the school relented and reluctantly transferred her to a regular class. But their problems were just beginning.

The girl didn't get a report card at the end of the first quarter. When the father called the school, he was told that his daughter was progressing well and would receive her report card later. Three more quarters passed, and they got no report card and the same answer. Finally the card came. The school gave the girl failing grades and transferred her back to the retarded class. The father was convinced the report card was fallacious, since he had been told his daughter was doing satisfactory work. Since the girl is now doing well in a private school, he probably was right.

"Avoid any confrontation with the educational bureaucracy," the father advised us, "and don't give in to their demands for either testing or placement. You just can't win."

We were grateful for our talk with these parents but depressed. Once again it drove home the point— if doctors or school officials label a child retarded, it's practically impossible to get them to admit their mistake and correct the situation.

Since Social Services hadn't contacted us directly, we didn't know who had ordered them to remove Jared from his school. Without giving my name, I phoned Social Services to find out under what conditions they'd go out to a school to remove a child.

The answer was quick and blunt. "We only go out to a school if the child's pediatrician notifies us that the child is retarded, or whatever, and belongs in a school for the handicapped."

"What's the procedure when you go to the school?" I asked.

"We physically take the child to a state regional center for testing and placement in a special school. And, sir, you're talking to the man who goes out to the school to do this."

Badly shaken, I hung up. It appeared that one of Jared's local pediatricians had contacted Social Services directly. It seemed to us that, through Social Services, he was trying to accomplish legally what he'd wanted to do in the first place—send Jared to a regional center for testing and placement. Despite Jared's recovery, we were back to square one.

A few weeks later we started getting newsletters from the local regional center. Marlene called them and asked how we got on their mailing list.

"Only a doctor can put you on our mailing list. It means you'll be using our services," the receptionist replied. Possibly Jared's name had gotten on the list by a routine action of the office staff who innocently filled out the state forms as a matter of course, but we feared it was another form of harassment.

We took Jared out of the private school. The director was under pressure from several sources now, and though she wasn't going to give in to Social Services, she probably was relieved when Jared left. Things had gotten so tense that keeping Jared there didn't seem worthwhile. Since kindergarten wasn't mandatory anyway, we planned to pick up Jared's education in the first grade. In our innocence, we thought things would change during the year, that we'd find a sympathetic doctor who'd diagnosis Jared's illness and help us get the retardation diagnosis changed.

Not long after Jared stopped going to school, we found there was no end to the retributions the medical system would demand because we had defied the diagnosis of its doctors. This time, it was David who became the target of an inhumane act by his own doctor.

It started one weekday morning, when David accidentally overturned a pot of boiling water in the kitchen, badly burning his arms. Screaming in pain, he yelled, "Mommy, Mommy, help me!" Marlene frantically started pulling his steaming shirt over his head, and as she did, the shirt rubbed lightly against one of his arms. When the shirt came off, she saw the skin on that arm had peeled away. David, gripped by a fear and pain he had never known, began shaking all over.

Marlene rushed him to his pediatrician's office, a few miles away. The nurse there casually remarked, "That was a good story you made up about your son Jared."

Marlene was speechless. Here was David in great pain, and the nurse was talking about a "story" we had never even told this pediatrician!

The nurse coldly led David into an examining room, told him to undress, and went out without saying another word. David was left sitting in his undershorts in a cold examining room, scared and crying in pain, while Marlene tried to comfort him.

Bewildered and frightened herself, Marlene kept going out to the nurse's station. "David's in pain. When will the doctor be treating him?" The nurse and receptionist looked past her and wouldn't answer. Two hours later, the doctor arrived. He examined David, then said curtly, "You'll have to go to a pharmacy and get your own burn ointment and bandages if you want me to treat David. I can't supply them."

Marlene was helpless. It was a heartless, senseless demand, but by this time she was willing to do anything to get relief for David and was forced to comply. She drove several blocks to a pharmacy, bought the ointment and bandages, and sped back to the doctor. Back at the office, she was immediately handed a slip of paper by the pediatrician and told sarcastically, "I'll need a special prescription burn ointment." She made another round trip, so enraged and burning with humiliation she could barely drive. This time, the doctor quickly and wordlessly bandaged David's wounds. The ordeal had lasted three hours.

The horror of what had been done to David was incomprehensible to us. What motive could turn a seemingly kind doctor into a monster? We wanted badly to believe there was a simple explanation for his behavior. We didn't want to be in a position where the unthinkable, the unreasonable, the senseless became reality.

We asked a friend to phone the doctor's office and got our answer the same day.

"I've just talked to the nurse," our friend said. "She says the doctor always stocks medical supplies for burn patients, and they have twenty-four-hour access to an emergency room at a hospital across the street."

I turned to Marlene. "My God! We're living in the twilight zone."

Jared at three months, healthy and happy.

David, Jared, and Marlene in 1974 just before Jared's illness began.

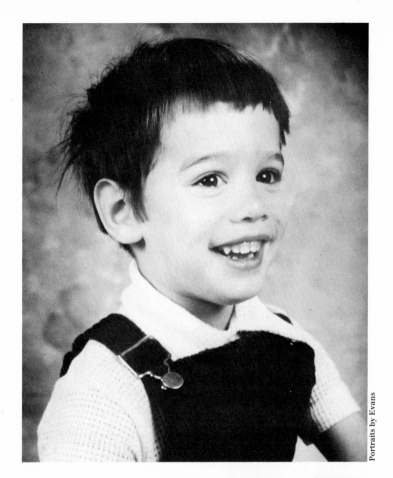

Who could guess the ordeal that would confront this beautiful three-year-old?

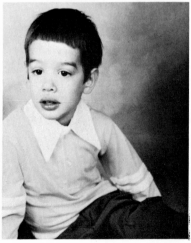

At age four Jared had been diagnosed as severely retarded or autistic and could not walk or talk.

Richard Gilmore

Our little guy has always been curious and loves to take things apart.

Barry Reisman

Jared, five, is finally free to go outside, as long as he wears the helmet built by Bruce Held of Lawrence Livermore National Laboratory.

Our whole family together at Disneyland in June 1982.

Richard Gilmore

*At six Jared's favorite toy was the water hose;
here he is wearing his space suit.*

March of Dimes

*Mischievous Jared takes aim at Dr. Raphael Wilson through the bubble
we use away from home and in hotels.*

Jared and his sister, Alicia, eyeball to eyeball.

An exercise bike and a whole set of indoor play equipment is one way we make sure Jared stays healthy and active.

Playing board games together is one of our family's favorite evening pastimes.

Sometimes it's impossible to pull Jared away from his computer.

Jared's an eager learner and Marlene's a stern teacher, so he spends plenty of time reading.

Jared, now twelve, is healthy and excited about the challenges of becoming a teenager.

7 Dr. Raphael Wilson, the "Bubble" Doctor

Fall 1977 had been one of the most traumatic times our family had experienced. Jared was threatened with institutionalization and barred from any real education, and the rest of us were seemingly denied medical care, even in an emergency. We knew what the doctor had done to David was probably illegal. His act was so bold and outrageous, he had to have an ulterior motive.

One thought we had was that he'd been trying to precipitate a confrontation with us. To have responded would have been futile. We were sure that, if we had gone to an attorney and filed suit, no judge or jury would have believed our accusations. The doctor was at the top of his profession and a member in good standing in his religious community. Also, a court case and bad publicity would have further alienated us from medical help. And, finally, the case could be used to prove to the press that we didn't get along with the medical community, which would cast even more doubt on our story. Like spies living in enemy territory, we had to move very cautiously.

As bad as things had been in September, our luck was about to change in one way. Jared needed new equipment so we could get him safely out of state for a complete medical examination. He needed a plastic bubble isolator for the car ride, for sleeping in a motel, for undergoing the examination. His plastic helmet and portable respirator, besides being uncomfortable for long periods, would have to be recharged throughout the day, an impossibility on the road. But Jared also needed an isolation garment to protect him from allergens and germs. Since he couldn't tolerate medications, protecting him from normal childhood illnesses was imperative.

As we had done so often before, we weighed all that had happened to us and decided to go back to medical professionals, hoping they might be able to define Jared's illness and, perhaps, help refute the retardation diagnosis. This time, though, we went out of state. I wrote to Baylor College of Medicine in Houston, asking for a medical exam and help in getting Jared the bubbles and protective suit.

Our first response was from the chairman of

Baylor's pediatric department, who said the technology we needed might be available through the NASA Space Center in Houston. He felt because of Jared's many difficulties, he required a complete evaluation by someone competent in the field and recommended "a good friend" of his, the medical director of the National Jewish Hospital in Denver. In closing, he offered to act as an intermediary if anything had to be worked out between Baylor and the space center.

We were very excited by the letter. I knew NASA had just built a space suit for David, the bubble boy. "It looks like we're finally on the right track," I told Marlene. "I have a gut feeling that this may be our breakthrough."

Baylor's pediatric chairman was as good as his word. He contacted NASA almost immediately, asked them to help us get new equipment for Jared, and for the next few months coordinated efforts to devise the equipment. He also got in touch with the director at the National Jewish Hospital, describing what was being attempted so that Jared could travel to Denver safely for a complete medical examination.

I started getting calls from scientists in the space program, some of them the same people I'd seen on TV during the Apollo moon shots between mid-1969 and late 1972. In the early sixties, when I had been an engineer at the Aerojet General Corporation, they had fabricated the service propulsion system engines for Apollo's lunar orbiter. The Apollo program's success had a special meaning for me, and I watched proudly as each mission was carried out. It was uncanny that I now was talking with Apollo's scientists about the technology involved in building a space suit for my own son.

People in NASA's biomedical applications section helped put us in touch with individuals and firms they felt might be able to provide the equipment Jared needed. Letters went back and forth for months, and finally came the news that they had found a manufacturer of plastic isolators. My letter was answered by the company president, who suggested that our first step should be to contact Dr. Raphael Wilson, in experimental biology at Saint Luke's Episcopal Hospital in Houston, the hospital that had been working with David, the bubble boy. The company had made most of David's chambers since before his birth, and the president said, once we had conferred with Dr. Wilson, he'd be happy to work with us.

The letter was the end of a long journey leading to the one man we felt could help us—Dr. Wilson. Looking back, we now realize all paths had been leading in that direction, ever since the local allergist speculated that some kind of purifier bubble might help Jared. But it was pure speculation at the time; the use of bubbles was so rare, few doctors knew how to get them.

Shortly after we got the good news about Dr. Wilson, Marlene and I learned just how necessary bubbles were to Jared's survival. We had taken five-year-old Jared on a short return trip to Disneyland and had brought along the large respirator designed for car and school use, plus a makeshift oxygen tent so he could sleep in the motel. In the middle of the night, while Jared's portable battery was recharging and the respirator was plugged into the motel wall socket, there apparently was a power surge in the electrical supply.

Jared's respirator stopped, and he reacted immediately with the all too familiar symptoms. His face swelled, and he became delirious. The portable battery unit had recharged just enough to give Jared some relief, but only two hours of battery time were left.

I called the emergency room at a hospital in Anaheim, my hands already shaking and panic welling up in me. A doctor there told me to phone the UCLA Medical Center, and the UCLA doctor told me to call the fire department paramedics for oxygen and to have Jared brought to the center as soon as possible. He wasn't sure the oxygen would be free of particulates, but he assumed it was.

Minutes after I called the fire department, two fire trucks and six firemen arrived. They rushed into our small motel room. Some began attending to Jared while others went to work trouble-shooting the equipment. As they were about to give up on the equipment and were getting ready to take Jared to the hospital, one of them cried out, "I've got it! It's a blown fuse." There was an all-night service station down the road. Much to my relief, they had the fuse I needed.

The equipment hummed back into operation. Marlene and I put Jared under the tent and spent most of the night watching over him. Gradually his swelling and pain subsided. Not only had he managed to get a few hours of sleep, by morning he had recovered enough to go to Disneyland. He went on many rides, and at the end of the day, finally exhausted and as happy as we'd ever seen him, he met Mickey Mouse. He was so excited to see him in person, he threw his arms around Mickey and gave him a big hug, and pressing his face against Mickey's he gave him a kiss through his mask.

For weeks Jared talked about the "wonderful" trip, but after the terrifying experience in the motel, all Marlene and I could think about was getting proper protective equipment for him so he could travel to be diagnosed and treated. We never wanted to be that scared again.

After Disneyland, we wrote to Dr. Wilson, describing Jared's medical history and asking for help. "Of course I'll help," he responded within days. He had been reading about Jared in the newspapers, he said, and was interested in taking on Jared's case. He believed the basis of Jared's illness probably was a genetic metabolic disorder.

The first time I spoke to Dr. Wilson on the phone, I was put at ease at once by his pleasant and reassuring voice. After discussing Jared for a while and making plans to meet, he told me he wanted to try to get a grant so he could start research on Jared's case, which, in turn, could help other children. "There must be other Jareds out there. Research into better diagnostic tools will help doctors when they see these cases."

I felt overwhelmed. A doctor had just told me Jared was not alone, that Jared and others could be helped. Marlene and I had always known it was possible.

We had to wait a few weeks while Dr. Wilson attended a conference on aging in Europe, but he called soon after he returned and asked to come visit us for a few days. I went to the airport to pick him up and knew him almost instinctively—distinguished, fiftyish, dressed in a business suit, wearing horn-rimmed glasses. He saw me looking at him and rushed over to shake my hand. "Hi, Barry. I recognized you from the newspapers."

On the drive home, I listened fascinated as he told me about his background as a professor of pediatrics at Baylor, where as a research immunologist he had designed the bubble isolators for David. He described with excitement how he had worked with NASA to create a miniature, germ-free space suit that allowed David to venture outside his isolator for the first time. To give me an idea of the work being done for children with immunological disorders, he had brought me a copy of one issue of the medical journal *Pediatric Research,* of which he was an associate editor. In it was a special report on a four-year study of his work with David.

Dr. Wilson went on to explain that he'd been one of the original doctors involved in bubble isolation technology. He told me there had been a recent TV documentary about children who live in plastic bubbles. My enormous surprise must have shown on my face as I learned there were other "bubble babies" throughout the world, that children with immune deficiency diseases had been placed in sterile bubble isolators to keep them alive until they either developed immune competence spontaneously or would be treated successfully. I was encouraged to hear that many of these children had developed immunity on their own and were able to leave their bubbles.

His new job as president of the University of

Portland allowed him some time for "moonlighting," he said, so along with his work with Jared, he was also doing research into the immunological disorders of the elderly.

Jared, wearing his headgear and backpack, was playing in the front yard when we got to the house. He had just found a treasure of coins on the sidewalk, which he gathered up and offered to the doctor, who said, "Well, Jared, it's nice to meet you. I'm not one to refuse money! Thank you so much." We all laughed.

Marlene came out to meet Dr. Wilson, and the three of us stayed outside for a while watching Jared dash madly about the yard, playing with his water toys and the garden hose. The doctor smiled—another bubble boy was running free, released from the isolation of his home. "It's just incredible, the similarities between Jared and David. Jared even looks like David," Dr. Wilson remarked as we went inside to talk.

It was a wonderful feeling to sit down in the privacy of our house and discuss Jared with a prominent immunologist. No cold offices or rushed doctors' schedules. It reminded me of when family doctors made home visits and kept up special relationships with their patients.

Dr. Wilson listened intently to our detailed account of Jared's medical history and the retardation diagnosis, then gave us his thoughts on the possible cause of his illness. "It appears to me that Jared has an inborn defect that makes his immune system work too actively on foreign substances he breathes into his body or that are absorbed through his skin."

The Houston boy's problem was at the opposite end of the spectrum from Jared's, he explained, for David had no immunity system at all, while Jared's was overactive.

"Even though their problems are at opposite ends of the spectrum, the effects are just as devastating. Before immune deficiency disease was recognized for what it was, children with the disease died of common infectious ailments like colds and pneumonia, without their doctors ever knowing why. It's my guess there probably have been many children with Jared's disease who've gone undiagnosed, then died from pneumonia, for example. In fact, Jared might be the only survivor."

Dr. Wilson's explanation was similar to the Mayo Clinic's. When the Mayo allergist phoned Marlene after our visit, she theorized that Jared was suffering from a rare immunological disorder. Since his blood tests revealed nothing abnormal, she thought the problem might be intracellular, complicated by mild allergies, but with something wrong in the cells that caused a devastating reaction. She felt another possibility was an autoimmune disease, a condition in which a person's white cells attack his own body. The allergist had left us with the chilling possibility that Jared might be one of those individuals with a one-of-a-kind illness that even Mayo wouldn't be able to diagnose.

"Is there any way to pin down what Jared has?" I asked Dr. Wilson.

"Jared's problem may be on an intracellular level...a missing enzyme. Blood tests might not show any abnormality, but more technologically advanced tests may be able to uncover the cause of his problem."

We explained that we'd recently been in touch with the director of the National Jewish Hospital in Denver, who also suspected Jared's illness was related to enzymes. Dr. Wilson felt that having Jared examined in Denver was the best course for us to take, and he urged us to do it. In the meantime, he said he'd check with research centers in California to see if they could take on Jared's case so we wouldn't have to travel so far. He felt sure prestigious research centers in the state wouldn't be influenced by what our local doctors had done.

Dr. Wilson stayed with us for two days. The biggest surprise of the visit came when we showed him Jared's equipment. It turned out that the High Efficiency Particulate Air (HEPA) filters were essentially the same used to keep "bubble" children alive. From the space program, the technology had spread simultaneously, though unevenly, in two different directions—to the medical and the industrial sectors. It was ironic that the industry people we had contacted were more aware of their equipment's medical potential than our own doctors.

We learned the history of isolation systems and about the variety of isolators being manufactured from Dr. Wilson. Turning to Jared's needs, he suggested we start with two plastic bubble isolators, one for car travel and a larger unit that would allow Jared to undergo medical examinations safely. Also, the doctor said he would contact NASA about fabricating a bubble-type helmet, similar to David's, that would give Jared better visibility and more comfort, because of its light weight. We measured the car for the isolator and Jared for the helmet.

Marlene and I spent several hours talking with Dr. Wilson about bubble children's physical, emotional, and intellectual development. We mentioned Jared's addiction to fast foods; the doctor cited recent studies that showed these foods had good nutritional value and the high calories an active, slender boy like Jared needed. We asked about discipline; the doctor smiled and said, "My personal philosophy is that bubble boys should never be spanked!"

It was proper physical development that was the doctor's chief concern. Since these children weren't totally free to go out in the world, special efforts had to be made to bring the world to them. Jared's helmet, for example, had that four-hour limit, and he couldn't wear it in the rain or in the winter. (The fan sucks outside air into the helmet. When the temperature falls, the air inside the helmet gets quite cold.) Dr. Wilson's recommendation was that we put a complete outdoor gym set with swings, climbing bars, and slides indoors, even if it took up a whole room.

We took that advice two weeks later, and it proved to be one of our best investments. All the children spent hours playing on the gym set. Every now and then, Jared would come to me, smiling, and say, "Daddy, I'm really lucky to have a playground in my room." And later we added a boxing bag and a basketball net that gave Jared and David healthy, active time together.

At the airport, as we were saying our good-byes to Dr. Wilson, thanking him for all his help and his attention and kindness to our family, he told us he felt very encouraged by his visit. "I feel Jared will someday overcome his illness and grow up to lead a normal life."

Marlene and I had a feeling of euphoria driving home, thinking about Jared's future, about finding a cure for his illness and someday seeing him running bareheaded like other children, able to breathe and thrive in fresh air and sunlight.

Dr. Wilson wrote a week later. He'd contacted the manufacturer, who said he would give top priority to producing Jared's bubbles. The doctor also was waiting to hear from NASA regarding the helmet. The closing of his letter moved us greatly. He said our strength of character, courage, and love were inspirational to observe and that these would be the key determinants in resolving Jared's problems and would also contribute to the welfare of many other children who suffer from conditions similar to Jared's.

We always knew Jared was a born survivor. Marlene said, if she were ever marooned on a desert island, she'd want Jared with her. He'd find a way to get them out. He seemed to have developed animal-like instincts for surviving, something we found out one hot summer afternoon.

Marlene was watering flowers in the front yard when two-year-old Alicia decided to cook a plastic wastebasket full of paper on the electric range. The smoke alarm went off, and Marlene rushed inside. Black smoke was pouring through the house. She started frantically searching for Jared and Alicia.

Marlene found five-year-old Jared taking a shower. One look at his mother's face, and he sensed immediately that he had to help her. He put on his undershorts, found his helmet, turned on the air flow, ran to Alicia's room where he found her sobbing, huddled in a corner, then calmly led her out of the smoke-filled house. Outside, he held her hand and comforted her until the firemen came and put out the fire.

Marlene called me at work, and I rushed home to find the firemen just cleaning up. They told me they'd had to turn off the blower that circulates filtered air throughout the house. The whole heating and cooling system was loaded with soot and would have to be professionally cleaned before we could turn it back on.

Then, right after the fire truck left, a large freight carrier pulled up to our house, and two delivery men began unloading a huge crate.

A month earlier we'd gotten a letter from the chief sales engineer at the company that built our house filters. He explained how pleased the company had been to read its name in a June 1978 *Los Angeles Times* article and to hear how its filters had helped Jared. A few weeks later a second letter came from the company, asking if we'd be interested in one of its commercial model air purifiers, one especially designed to remove submicron particles, thus making the air in our house even cleaner for Jared. We wrote back right away that we'd be delighted to have the new unit.

"Barry, it's our new air filtering system," Marlene yelled as she opened the door for the delivery men.

"Oh, my God! Just on the night we can't use our house filters!"

"It's another miracle," Marlene said.

I had the men set up the unit, which was very heavy and larger than a washing machine, in the den. Then I turned it on. Air blew out of it with such force that, standing in front of it, I felt like I was in a hurricane. My hair was literally standing up. "Marlene, this should really keep our house clean. You may never have to dust again."

That night we moved Jared's bed into the den. He slept there for a few nights. For him, sleeping there, watching TV, and eating off TV trays was as much fun as camping out.

Over the next few days, the soot-blackened house became a work site, as tradesmen came and went, scrubbing down walls, removing drapes for cleaning, shampooing rugs and furniture, painting rooms. Alicia and Jared spent their days roaming from room to room, watching wide-eyed as the men worked. A few times, the workmen stopped and let the thrilled children help mix paint and straighten out drop cloths. Alicia and Jared missed the men when the house finally was put in order and talked about them for weeks after.

All through the summer of 1978, Dr. Wilson worked to get the bubbles for Jared, while NASA engineers stepped in to find a protective suit. Jared needed such a suit to keep his skin from absorbing airborne allergens. We knew he could get sick anytime, especially in dense wooded areas, even with protective breathing gear. On our trip to Denver, we would be traveling through many new areas, each with an unknown exposure risk. Dr. Wilson and I concurred. We had to find a way to control that risk, so Jared could stay well on the trip to Denver.

NASA, in turn, contacted the National Institute of Health, which previously had been involved in developing and testing isolation garments for certain high-risk patients at its National Cancer Institute. Those patients, who'd had radiation and cytotoxic drug therapy, were highly susceptible to infection, for the therapy affected their immune systems.

NCI put these patients in portable laminar-airflow rooms provided with special air filters that maintained a positive pressure by pumping excess filtered air into the room, much like Jared's portable head bubble. The result was that excess clean air flowed out of the room, but no "dirty" outside air could leak in. These patients spent long periods in their sterile laminar-airflow rooms, but, of course, they had to leave their rooms periodically for a change of surroundings or for medical reasons such as therapy or x-rays. Thus arose the need for a mobile sterile environment, a bacteriological isolation garment and filtered air supply. The garment, developed collaboratively by NCI, NASA, and Arthur D. Little, Inc., was comfortable, convenient to use, and safe, for it let a patient leave the laminar-airflow room without compromising his or her isolation.

Just a few years after clinical use at NCI, these protective suits would be worn by the astronauts upon returning from the first moon landing. The suits prevented the spread of unknown diseases NASA feared might be brought back from the moon, by quarantining the astronauts after their mission.

A physician in charge of pediatric oncology at the National Cancer Institute gave me the names of the companies that manufactured the suit fabric and the finished suit. The fabric, called BAR-BAC, was a dense, woven broadcloth, ideal for a protective suit, because it would keep out particles larger than .03 microns.

Getting the suit became my "project." I felt somewhat like a graduate student in the middle of a master of science thesis, like several years earlier at Drexel University, when I designed and built an experimental distillation apparatus. The situation was different, but some things were the same. I was left to my own initiative, working with the best information I could find for a result that wasn't guaranteed.

My conversation with the suit fabricator in Cambridge, Massachusetts, went smoothly. I spoke with a woman there named Marlene, a chemical engineer, who told me that, besides manufacturing suits for NASA, the company had made one for a high school boy with aplastic anemia. She gave me the details of the suit. It was a loose, front-zippered coverall with mittens and double-soled slippers attached to the garment, and all seams were made with a blind-hem stitch to cut down on leakage. An external hood or head bubble attached to the body of the suit to make it airtight, and filtered air was mechanically pumped into the suit at the back of the neck, puffing up the dense fabric, while air flowed out through openings in the fabric. Since positive air pressure was maintained at all times inside the suit, outside air was prevented from leaking in.

I told her the suit sounded wonderful and asked if the company could make one for Jared.

"Yes, we certainly can, but we have some pro-
duction backlogs. It could take several months."
When I told her I had to get the suit as soon as possible, so Jared could travel to Denver, she promised
to send me complete specifications for the suit right
away.

I found a seamstress in town who was anxious to
tackle the unusual job of making a space suit, and I
called the fabric manufacturer in St. Louis and ordered several yards of material. Two weeks later the
fabric arrived. It was powder blue, Jared's favorite
color. We were one step closer to Denver.

The space suit was finished in two weeks, and
soon after that we received the two bubble isolators,
as well as a clear plastic helmet, for the suit. Funds
from the northern California section of the March of
Dimes had paid for all the equipment. It was now
August 1978, and our plans were to try to get Jared
enrolled in first grade in September, then make the
trip to Denver in January 1979.

When Dr. Wilson came to our house to inspect
and instruct us in the use of the isolators and suit,
the event was heralded by a press conference and
filmed by the national TV show, "America Alive."
The house was filled with a dozen reporters, cameramen, photographers, and representatives from the
March of Dimes.

At the press conference, Jared, dressed in his
new space suit, asked the doctor, "Can I get a real
rocket, too?"

"I'm sorry, Jared. NASA doesn't have a rocket for
you, but I promise I'll get you a NASA patch for your
space suit, okay?" Jared nodded energetically and
ran outside in his new suit to ride his bike and kick

the paper-dry autumn leaves along the sidewalk. The cameras followed him.

Inside our bedroom, the new sleeping bubble was being inflated. Bright lights flooded the scene and cameras began rolling again as Jared climbed into his bubble for the first time.

Squealing and giggling inside the bubble, he squirted his water pistol at Dr. Wilson and the reporters. The spirit of the event was so high, the doctor had a hard time keeping himself from laughing while he explained the medical uses of bubbles to the national audience. Finally, the whole room just broke out in laughter. Seeing the futility of trying to maintain seriousness, Dr. Wilson got his revenge on Jared by tickling him through the bubble, proving that strong vinyl can withstand the antics of a rambunctious little boy, and that "isolation" is a relative thing.

8

Report Cards and the Media

Now it was time to focus on Jared's education. I had recently seen a TV ad announcing the opening of a new parochial school. Its campus looked spacious, and the idea of a good academic program in a warm, Christian atmosphere appealed to us. Also, the school went through twelfth grade, and we thought it could be ideal for Jared and David, and eventually Alicia, to be at the same school and not have to change after grade school.

The school superintendent invited Marlene and

me to come out and see him the same day I called. We found the campus even more impressive than on the TV ad. It looked like a college campus, with the main building that housed the classrooms surrounded by smaller buildings for the gym, wood shop, and other activities.

The superintendent, a tall, scholarly-looking man, radiated enthusiasm about the new school. He had just given up his position as superintendent in another California county, he told us, in order to pursue a Christian-oriented approach to education. We liked the man at once, and with his background and Ph.D. in education and a ministerial degree, we knew he was the kind of educator we wanted to entrust with our children's education.

David had always been an A student, so the superintendent accepted him with no questions for the fifth grade. Then I explained Jared's medical problem and showed him the portable respirator. The superintendent's first concern was setting up an environment in which Jared could interact freely with his classmates and his teacher, a situation that wasn't possible when Jared was confined to the respirator.

"We have a spare classroom," he said. "Could you arrange to have it equipped with an air-filtering system? The school could help out with the installation. I think it's important for Jared to have a room he could share with a few other first graders, with the teacher going back and forth between the rooms."

"That would be perfect," I said. "In fact, the manufacturer who supplied our house filters just wrote us and offered to send us a large filtering machine for a classroom at no charge."

The superintendent explained that, before we went ahead with any arrangements, he wanted to discuss Jared's admission with the school's board members and faculty. "We're meeting this Thursday night. I'll let you know their decision on Saturday."

Our meeting with the superintendent had gone better than we ever could have imagined. We never dreamed of Jared in a classroom free of his portable equipment, sitting at his own desk, talking, teasing, playing games, doing art projects, running around the room, fighting with other boys, learning the social play rules of childhood.

Early Saturday morning the phone rang. I knew from the tone of the superintendent's voice that the news was good.

"Our board and faculty are unanimously in favor of accepting Jared. We all feel it's our Christian duty to educate and guide him." We thanked him and told him how sincerely grateful we were for the decision. "Now, it'll take a few weeks to prepare the special classroom for Jared," he said. "In the meantime, we'd like to start him on a home study program. Why don't you come in next week to meet Jared's new teacher?"

She was a smiling, friendly woman in her mid-forties, surrounded by a spacious and well-equipped classroom that soon would be filled with children. "I'm really looking forward to having Jared as a student. It will be a real challenge, and a real joy. It's students like Jared who make teaching worthwhile."

She outlined her plans for Jared's integration

into the class. At first, he would begin school on the home study program, but she also wanted him to come to school three afternoons a week for two hours. "These visits to school will be important. They'll give him the socialization he needs. He'll even have his own desk, so he'll feel like he's part of the class."

Next she described the first grade curriculum and gave us Jared's reading, writing, spelling, and arithmetic texts and workbooks. "We use the Open Court Correlated Language Arts Program here," she said, showing us the reading workbook. "It's an advanced phonetic approach to reading, writing, and spelling. Actually, our whole curriculum is probably one of the most advanced in the area. By the end of the first grade, the children can read almost anything and can write compositions. I've found that, when children learn all the fundamentals in the first grade, they rarely have learning problems later." At the end of our meeting, the teacher told us to bring Jared to class the day school opened, so he could meet his classmates and be assigned his desk.

Marlene leafed through the workbooks on our way home, noticing the spelling words—"physician," "patient," "musician"—and the multiplication and fractions exercises in the math book. "Barry, do you think we've made a mistake? After all Jared's been through and only starting to talk a year and a half ago, is it fair to put him in an advanced class where he'll have to work so hard to keep up with the other kids?"

I tried to reassure her. "Remember how he learned to speak by learning the phonetic sounds you taught him? Remember the arithmetic workbooks he did on his own? I think he'll do just fine!"

Marlene and I took six-year-old Jared to school that first morning. He was wearing his blue helmet. As soon as we walked into the noisy classroom, the fifteen children who had been busy talking and playing converged on Jared. "Where'd you get that Star Wars costume?" they asked in unison. The teacher came over and put her arm around Jared.

"Children, this is Jared. He'll be in this class with you. He wears this special helmet to protect him because he has allergies. Just like some of you have to wear glasses, Jared has to wear his helmet."

Unlike the children in his kindergarten class who just accepted Jared without question, the first graders, older and more worldly wise, bombarded him with questions, which he bashfully answered. "How do you sleep?" "What happens if you turn the motor off?" "Can you take a shower?" And, as always, "Where can I get a helmet like yours?"

The teacher let the questioning go on for a while, then showed Jared to his desk and called the class to order. On that first day she introduced the class to the phonetic sounds of some of the alphabet. Jared took the whole scene very seriously. He sat engrossed during a writing assignment, and when one girl tried to talk to him, he said, "Don't bother me, I'm busy."

We were very happy Jared had done so well the first day and relieved he'd been so readily accepted by the other children. His eyes sparkled with excitement. "Mommy, I really like school!" We celebrated the occasion by stopping at Jared's favorite eatery—

McDonald's—where he downed two hamburgers, french fries, and a chocolate milk shake. To avoid allergens, we had to quickly slip Jared his food through the helmet's drawstring opening.

Jared started on the home study program, with the assignments his teacher gave Marlene each week. He did the same work his classmates were doing in school, and the teacher graded his work along with the other students'. On the afternoons he went to school, the teacher scheduled workbook assignments Jared could do at his desk without her direction—since, because of his helmet, he couldn't hear her at the front of the room—as well as art projects that allowed Jared to work and socialize with other children.

Contrary to Marlene's fears, Jared thrived on the advanced program. He learned to read and write and soared ahead of his classmates so quickly the teacher had to give him extra work. Arithmetic was his favorite subject. He finished the first grade book and was advanced to the second and third.

Working alone on his math in the evenings, he taught himself multiplication and division and took every opportunity to show off his math skills on days when he went to school. When the teacher sent the children to the blackboard to do addition and subtraction problems, Jared, during his turn, proudly and mischievously changed a plus or a minus sign to a multiplication sign and proceeded to multiply the numbers. As his teacher watched, delighted, and his classmates stared, amazed, Jared stood back from the board and grinned with satisfaction.

His interest in numbers sometimes ran to the

more serious, almost theoretical aspect of mathematics, and he'd ask his teacher, "What is the largest number?" "Do numbers ever end?" "Do numbers go back to zero?" "How do you write numbers that are less than zero?" The teacher always did her best to answer him.

Jared's fanciful side also emerged during this time, stimulated by his contact with other children and exposure to new books at school. He kept a large collection of ghost stories and tried to re-create the haunted houses he read about by draping sheets over the furniture in his room. Anyone walking past his room was threatened by haunting ghost sounds from beneath the sheets. Even when he didn't really "get" us, we pretended to scream in terror, which sent Jared into uproarious giggling.

And Jared was now healthier than he had ever been. Marlene's mother, proud of her scholarly grandson, made sure he got plenty of nutritious, homemade food. Every day, she came to our house to prepare a delicious Russian meal, high in calories and full of good things for the body and soul. Jared's all-time favorite was stewed chicken with matzo-ball soup and lemon meringue pie. Marlene, her mother, and I, recalling earlier times when Jared had trouble lifting a fork to his mouth, watched in pleasure as he devoured his meals with gusto.

When the first rains came that fall, Marlene was in the park with Jared. He ran to the car, took off his helmet, and laid it on the car floor. Then, smiling, he stepped into the rain and dashed to the slide. At the top he stopped for a moment, long enough to let Marlene catch sight of a Jared she had forgotten ever existed. In his jeans and burgundy shirt, black hair wet and free to the wind, his big brown eyes shining, he was a picture of absolute health and happiness. Marlene had the momentary feeling of having a dead child coming back to be with her for a short while. She started to cry. This was the Jared who might have been, who she had imagined when he was born, who, through illness, we had been robbed of.

Six weeks into the school term, Jared's teacher called Marlene aside and told her, "The superintendent just notified me that we are dropping the plans for the special classroom."

"Why? Why are you changing your plans?"

"We're going to be moving in two years, and we don't think it's worthwhile to set up a special classroom."

Marlene could feel the color rising in her cheeks. "Why would moving affect setting up the classroom? The equipment's portable and won't require any permanent change in the room."

The teacher politely repeated what the superintendent had told her. Marlene's mind raced. Could someone have contacted the school staff and put pressure on them not to cooperate with us? We talked it over that night and decided the change of plans wasn't sufficient evidence to suggest the worst and that we wouldn't question the teacher further.

But two weeks later, when the first report card was due, Jared didn't get one. Marlene asked the teacher for it and was told, "Jared doesn't need a report card. You're his teacher. You can make one up for him. And you can also start correcting his homework yourself."

So it had happened again. We felt that, since

Jared's academic achievements probably posed a direct threat to the retardation diagnosis, there would be an effort to stop his education. With no report card and no graded homework, there was no record of Jared's performance in school, and the idea that he wasn't a normal student could be perpetuated. And, by making it so difficult for us to properly educate Jared, the school was, in effect, trying to force us out. It seemed to be a transparent attempt at expulsion.

Outside pressure had to be the reason for the school's actions. Had the superintendent been acting on his own, he would have called us in to meet with the teachers and board and given us a legitimate reason for expelling Jared.

The school's handbook outlined the expulsion procedure clearly. It stated that, in cases of irreconcilable differences between parents and the school, the school reserved the right to dismiss the student. So we didn't complain and didn't argue. That way we knew the school couldn't legally expel Jared. Its only recourse was to intimidate and harass us into leaving. We were determined not to let that happen.

That the teacher who knew Jared's skills so well and the clergymen at this Christian school could participate in such an act toward an innocent child was beyond belief. We remembered snatches of conversation: "... our Christian duty to educate and guide him" and "... students like Jared who make teaching worthwhile." All concepts of morality lay forgotten.

Just as things were reaching a crisis at the school, in-depth stories on Jared appeared in *McCalls, Family Circle,* and *Family Weekly* magazines.

Months before, Marlene and I had decided to tell the press the whole story of Jared's misdiagnosis—the part we had omitted in earlier interviews with newspaper and magazine reporters. Because we hadn't thought it appropriate for patients to air their grievances against doctors publicly, we had been willing to try to forgive and to forget what was being done to Jared. But when Social Services went to Jared's kindergarten and harassed the school director, we stopped forgiving. And we knew we'd never forget.

Telling the media seemed our only hope, if we were to keep the authorities at bay and thwart their efforts to get Jared away from us. They wouldn't be so bold as to fight us in the press, we were sure, for in doing so they'd expose their own incompetence. Our doctors would look ludicrous if they told the press that a happy, intelligent boy belonged in an institution. If they removed Jared's equipment, he would get critically ill, and the doctors would risk showing the world they could do nothing to help him.

The doctors couldn't accuse us of lying to the press, either. We had all the documentation to support what had happened—records of visits to doctors, results of tests showing Jared highly allergic to most airborne substances, tests run at the Mayo Clinic and correspondences with doctors there, the receipt for a hearing aid prescribed by an otologist, and, finally, our pediatrician's handwritten referral to a state regional center for testing and placement in a facility.

So we decided to talk on record. We wrote to the three magazines, to the *San Francisco Chronicle* and the *Los Angeles Times*—we didn't contact our local papers. Within a few weeks, stories on Jared appeared in the two papers and were carried over the international wire services. The articles covered Jared's strange illness, our doctors' diagnosis and inability to come up with an effective treatment, and our struggle to save Jared's life.

Soon after these stories appeared, we began to suspect just how threatened the medical community felt by the publicity and how actively they may have been trying to stop it. I had gone to buy a new battery pack for Jared's outdoor equipment and mentioned to the sales representative that Jared's story soon would be in three national magazines. I thought he'd be pleased. His company had voluntarily furnished Bruce Held the parts for the outdoor equipment, and its name had been mentioned in newspaper articles. We had even received a letter from the company's former western regional manager, the same man who had earlier given so generously of his time and services in donating the filtering equipment for Jared's helmet. He wrote: "My mother always told me that life's greatest gift is the joy of giving. Your boy's happiness is a priceless gift to me in my retirement."

As soon as I mentioned the coming magazine coverage, the sales representative awkwardly excused himself and hurried to the phone. Though he didn't know it, I could hear him leaving a message with his home office to call him back. Then he put down the phone, walked over to me, and said sternly, "My company doesn't want to have any part of your story. I've just called the home office to tell them about the articles. They'll be calling the magazines to stop the articles from appearing."

Nearly crying, I pleaded, "Please don't do this!

Jared's survival depends on those articles. The doctors want to stop the publicity, so their retardation diagnosis isn't exposed."

"You have to realize, my job is at stake here."

"Why would you want to do something that would hurt my son? You can't imagine what we've gone through to keep him alive! I heard you on the phone. Since your company doesn't know about the articles yet, and we're not going to tell them you know, why do you have to worry about your job?"

I must have moved him. "Okay, okay, I won't tell them. But I think you should see this." He showed me a company memorandum that said Jared was not supposed to be using the equipment, and we were not to be sold any more equipment, including the battery pack. Despite this, I got the salesman to sell me the pack. Given the turn of events, it was a small victory.

My God, I thought, now the doctors are trying to interfere with Jared's access to his equipment. Their maliciousness knew no bounds.

The magazine articles came out in October. All three carried details of the doctors' retardation diagnosis and their attempts to institutionalize Jared. Two magazines had asked for the names of the key doctors, including Jared's original pediatrician, so they could contact them and give them a chance to tell their side of the story. If the doctors talked, we were told, their version of the story would be printed along with ours. But if the doctors refused to comment, both magazines said they would assume our version was correct. The articles came out with no rebuttal from any doctor.

The coverage of our story was extensive, more than we had hoped for, a permanent documentation on Jared's illness and how it was brought under control. If there were other children out there suffering from symptoms similar to Jared's, the articles would encourage parents and doctors not to give up hope. Today, years later, we still are grateful to the magazine editors who believed our story and had the courage to print it.

At the time the magazines were on the newsstands, six-year-old Jared had his first exposure to the real world of mental retardation. One afternoon, two large vans pulled into the parking lot of our neighborhood park, where Marlene took Jared and Alicia every day. Two attendants dressed in white got out of each van, opened the back doors, pulled down the ramps and started wheeling severely brain-damaged adults into the park. Most of the patients were strapped into their wheelchairs, and most were staring vacantly as the attendants talked to them softly and comforted those who were crying.

Marlene felt Alicia and Jared were too young to comprehend such severe disabilities in adults, so she took their hands and started to leave the park. But Jared already had spotted the wheelchairs. He ran over to the patients, bent down by one wheelchair ·and began feeling the wheels. "Where did you get this chair? Can you walk? Can I sit in your chair?" The man Jared was talking to never even lifted his head, and he didn't respond. Jared said good-bye nonchalantly and walked back to where Marlene was waiting with Alicia.

Jared said nothing about the incident until they

got home. Then he started questioning Marlene. "Why were the people in the park sitting in those chairs?"

"Because they can't walk," she answered.

"Why can't they walk? Why can't they talk?"

"Sometimes people get hurt in their heads, and then they can't walk or talk too well."

"No, Mommy. That's not right. I saw it on TV. You get that way 'cause your mommy smoked and didn't eat right before you were born, right? I'm glad you eat right."

Jared took such a matter-of-fact attitude toward what he had seen. He seemed so sure of his normalcy. It was a great relief to us. Eventually, we knew, he'd learn that he once had been diagnosed as retarded, and when that day came, he'd need all the self-assurance and strength he could muster.

9 *The Deadly Game Continues: National Jewish Hospital*

We started getting ready to leave for Denver in high spirits, dampened only slightly by some strange incidents the month before. On Christmas Eve, Marlene got a phone call from a woman who identified herself as a "National Jewish Hospital informant" and said we would be put in our place when we went to Denver, that Jared's case, including the publicity, "was a laugh." She also said, "One of your allergists is a former colleague of the medical director at NJH." She named the allergist and challenged us to "go ahead and ask the director."

We received a few anonymous phone calls, too, warning us we were in grave danger and would need protection in Denver. We dismissed all these as crank calls and felt the "informant's" suggestion about the NJH director preposterous. For almost a year we'd been corresponding with the director, who was very excited about our upcoming visit. He had told us and the press he suspected Jared's illness might be caused by a rare enzyme error that keeps the body from processing the products of a normal allergic response. There had never been a case reported like it, he told the *San Francisco Chronicle* and *Family Weekly* magazine, and the diagnosis would be a completely new discovery.

Several days before we left for Denver, Dr. Wilson called us. "I'm scheduled to be in Denver myself during the week of January 20th, so I'll be seeing you!" He offered to oversee Jared's examinations at NJH and help familiarize the doctors there with Jared's bubbles. NJH was anxious to see Jared and name his rare disease, he said, and the doctors were also greatly interested in our environmental equipment.

It was a cold, dreary morning the day we started our trip. We had gotten up at dawn and found the press already waiting patiently outside in the front yard. We had no idea who had called them. Every now and then the reporters peered through the windows to see if we were ready. We packed the car and got Jared, half-asleep, into his car bubble. He was startled but good-natured about the cameras and TV reporters converging on him to cover the departure.

Just a few hours into our trip, a suitcase with all

my clothes in it fell off the luggage rack and was lost. It was an awful way to start off, but it had a happy ending. A kind gentleman from Lodi, California, found the suitcase on the road and traced it to me. It was in Denver when we got there, and inside it was a $50 bill and a note: "Good luck, Jared. We're all rooting for you." He wasn't the only well-wisher. En route to Denver, we saw the coverage of our departure in the newspapers and on TV. Later we got clippings and good luck wishes from as far away as France and Germany.

The trip took three days on clear but somewhat slippery roads. We just missed a snowstorm in Wyoming that left cars and trucks overturned in snow drifts on the side of the road. The whole time Jared's bubble, occupying the entire back seat of our car, worked perfectly. Relaxed and content, he played happily in there with his new toys, especially with a large stuffed turtle he pretended to feed and care for. Jared asked endless questions as we drove through the countryside.

At mealtimes we stopped and got takeout foods that we quickly slipped to Jared through the zippered opening in his car bubble. When we were parked, we often left the rear hatch door open so Jared could enjoy the new surroundings and talk with passersby who would stop, amazed, and chat with him through the plastic bubble. In the afternoons he took long naps, wrapped in his favorite blanket.

The startling winter scenery in the mountain states was the highlight of the trip for six-year-old Jared, who was seeing snow for the first time. "The mountains look like they're covered with cheese cake, and it's making me hungry!" he shouted, exhilarated. We stopped often, at Jared's pleading, so he could get out of his bubble and into his space suit to play in the snow. He romped happily; we threw snowballs and built a snowman—normal delightful fun, just like any boy with his mom and dad.

In the motel room at night, I connected a special monitor to the bubble so Jared could sleep in it safely. The monitor is an electronic relay-switching device that sounds an alarm if the power fails or the bubble collapses for any reason. The alarm would wake us so we could connect a battery-powered backup respirator to the bubble. Once the monitor was connected, Marlene climbed into the forty-five-cubic-foot bubble with Jared and helped him do his schoolwork assignments, so he wouldn't fall behind. On this trip, there were no alarms; Jared slept long and comfortably every night.

It was Sunday night when we got to Denver. We checked into a motel across the street from the hospital, had a good night's sleep, and early the next morning ate a huge breakfast. Earlier we had explained to Jared the purpose of our trip and the possibility that the doctors might find a cure for his illness. Now we walked across the street for our 10:00 A.M. appointment, all of us excited and anticipating a new life without the bubbles.

Marlene and I immediately knew something was wrong. We were met at the hospital by a public relations man, who introduced us to our doctors. They seemed nervous and uneasy and gave us a cold welcome. As I shook hands with one of them, he asked, "Why did you come here? What do you want?"

We were paralyzed. These were the same doctors with whom we had been corresponding and planning our trip. They had even recommended the motel where we were staying.

I must have stammered something, but one doctor said, out of the blue, "We must squash this publicity once and for all." I was bewildered, half-frantic, and bitterly disappointed. What the hell was going on here? How could we go through this again?

Then came the final blow. The doctors said they wanted to take Jared out of his bubble and give him IQ and hearing tests—nothing else. "We'll take him out of his bubble tomorrow," a doctor announced curtly, without even asking about Jared's possible reaction to unfiltered air.

Everything fell into focus. We theorized that our local doctors had already contacted NJH doctors, how long before we got to Denver we didn't know. As we listened in disbelief, the NJH doctor gave us the same diagnosis, word for word, as our local allergist. Jared's illness appeared to be caused by nothing more than allergic rhinitis combined with retardation. Also, they seemed to believe that Jared couldn't take any stress, even going outside, without falling apart. The impossible had happened. The informant was right.

I decided to confront the director. Had our allergist been in touch with him, I asked. He refused to answer. I repeated the question. Again he wouldn't answer. It's a close-knit fraternity, I knew, and it seemed doctors would protect their own.

We felt that, if the doctors could have just shuffled us out the door, they would have. They were upset about the seventeen press calls they'd received that morning. But they couldn't just shuffle off the press, either. The public relations man scheduled a news conference for that afternoon.

Marlene and I walked into the press conference holding Jared's hands. A staff physician followed us into the room, which was packed with photographers and reporters from four TV stations, United Press International, Associated Press, and several newspapers. Jared was in his space suit, full of spunk and energy, unaware of what had happened that morning. He aimed and shot his water pistol at the photographers. There were laughs all around as Jared and photographers traded "shots." Jared hadn't heard the doctor say to Marlene, as we'd stepped into the room, "Get out there, actress!" Neither had the press.

All we could think was that the doctors, from the moment we'd arrived, had been trying to break us down so at the press conference we'd come out "swinging," complaining and making accusations. Then all they would have to do was deny our story about what they had said in the morning, and we would look like crazy, ranting parents. Who would the press believe, us or these highly esteemed professionals? We were in enemy territory, again.

The press conference began. With great self-assurance the doctors told the press they would be doing blood and skin tests and taking x-rays in an attempt to diagnose Jared's illness.

The conference lasted half an hour. During it, we tried to relax and smile. We weren't going to let the doctors break us down and "get" us in front of the press. We answered the reporters' questions as though the morning's events had never happened.

Q: "Mr. Reisman, how has living in a bubble affected Jared?"

A: "So far, life inside the bubble hasn't affected him noticeably. We try to give him as normal a life as possible."

Q: "How's Jared doing in school, and how do his classmates react to him?"

A: "Jared has adapted well to school, and he's received well by his classmates. He's happy and bright."

Q: "Did you bring any other bubble besides the car bubble?"

A: "We brought along a forty-five-cubic-foot bubble for Jared to use in motel rooms. Yesterday his mother got into it with him, and they did two hours of school work."

Q: "How long do you expect to stay in Denver?"

A: "I have utmost confidence in the doctors here. We'll stay in Denver as long as it takes."

The game went on, and I could only hope the doctor sitting next to me was squirming inwardly. When the conference ended, he walked past me coldly and left the room without saying a word. The next day coverage of the conference was on the front pages of the *Rocky Mountain News* and the *Denver Post* and had gone out over both wire services.

That evening at the motel, we were too angered by the day's events to even think of going to sleep. Instead, we stayed up all night thinking through what had happened and trying to decide how to safely handle the situation. The doctors had told us they believed mental retardation to be the cause of Jared's illness. When Marlene pointed out that Jared was doing well in the first grade with an advanced curriculum, that his teachers found he caught on to new concepts faster than the average child, the doctors, unmoved, responded that IQ tests alone would determine if Jared was retarded.

All right, we decided. Since they were so adamant about the IQ test, we would agree to go ahead with it. If they gave Jared a "real" test, unskewed, we were pretty sure the results would settle the retardation issue once and for all and maybe even encourage these doctors to go ahead with the immunological tests. Jared desperately needed medical care, and we'd do anything to help him get it.

The next morning I phoned the doctor and told him we wanted to go ahead with the IQ test, provided it would be administered inside Jared's bubble. The doctor hung up on me. I phoned back and he hung up again. Marlene and I conferred quickly and came to the same conclusion. It was futile for us to remain at NJH.

I called the hospital's public relations man and told him why we would be leaving Denver. We told him the whole story, but, of course, he already knew the details. Marlene and I didn't want our abrupt departure to provide fuel for what seemed to us to be an evil game, so we agreed to a joint statement with the hospital that the public relations man would issue to the press later that day. This was the statement we agreed on: "By mutual agreement, we are terminating Jared's care at National Jewish Hospital, because they cannot conduct Jared's tests inside the bubble. We do not want to risk taking him out of the bubble."

We packed almost feverishly, then made one

more call before leaving Denver. We'd missed linking up with Dr. Wilson, because he was scheduled to be in Denver on the third day of our visit. I reached him at home, and as I told him what happened, he listened quietly and expressed great disappointment at the unexpected turn of events. But there wasn't much he could say or do. In a voice that trailed off, he said, "Evidently they believe the stress theory as the cause of Jared's illness." Later he wrote to say how sorry he was that we had been put through such trauma in Denver, and how he regretted not having been with us from the first, as liaison between us and the NJH doctors.

We left Denver and soon after found that NJH's public relations man had not issued our statement to the press. In an Associated Press story, a hospital spokesman was quoted as saying we didn't show up on Tuesday for a second visit and that only later had we notified the hospital we'd withdrawn Jared. Another article quoted a spokesman as saying NJH didn't know why we'd left. And, in yet another, a staff physician told the reporter he wanted to conduct hearing tests outside the bubble, that "We would have liked to have helped this kid."

As horrible as our Denver trip had been, when we got home, we still faced the problem of Jared's school withholding his report card. Without that academic documentation, the doctors could protect their retardation diagnosis from scrutiny. Its absence was a powerful weapon for them.

The battle lines had been drawn, but soon we were to win one important skirmish. For months after we returned from Denver, I kept requesting the report card. The school finally relented. In April we got Jared's first report card—all A's. At the end of the school year, Jared's teacher gave him a SAT test, on which he scored high, at the third-grade level.

Armed with the report card, letters from NJH showing that they had invited Jared to Denver for diagnostic tests in his bubble, letters from the Mayo Clinic, and continued press coverage, we knew we were still ahead in our struggle to protect Jared.

About a year and a half after Denver, we sent copies of the NJH letters and itemized medical receipts from Mayo to some reporters. Not long afterward, NJH sent us a bill for services they never performed. The bill showed a previous balance and amount due. We were shocked and insulted to receive the bill, because it gave the impression that Jared was examined at Denver. Perhaps NJH was trying to document an examination that had never taken place, even though they admitted in a newspaper article that they hadn't examined Jared. I wrote to them twice and asked what the charges were for, but they never replied. Marlene and I were appalled at the lengths doctors would go in order to maintain a diagnosis.

10 *Typical Days*

A few days before Jared began second grade, Marlene got a call from a producer at a TV station in Buenos Aires. In a heavy Spanish accent, he explained that his station wanted to do a one-hour segment on Jared for their program "60 Minutes"—the Argentine equivalent of CBS's program of the same name. Jared's story, he said, would become part of the international celebration of the Year of the Child. Marlene, delighted and honored that a TV crew from so far away was interested in Jared, accepted readily.

On Labor Day weekend the English-speaking hostess of the show and her cameraman, just off a twelve-hour flight from Argentina, arrived at our house in the taxi they'd hired for the whole time they'd be in Sacramento. They wanted to do nothing special, they said. They just would film our family doing what we did on a typical weekend, interviewing us informally along the way.

For the next three days, they followed us to our regular haunts. At the park, they filmed Jared and Alicia riding the merry-go-round and the miniature railroad and later tried to keep up with the children as they ran around the zoo, feeding peanuts to the monkeys and elephants and chasing squirrels.

The crew treated seven-year-old Jared to a shopping spree at a toy store on their last day of filming, then shot more footage as the hostess interviewed Jared playing with his booty. When she asked what he wanted to be when he grew up, Jared paused a moment, grinned mischievously, and answered, "I'd like to be a kid forever and play with toys!" Considering he had just had three days of attention and Christmas in September, Marlene and I weren't surprised he loved life the way it was.

Jared was filmed putting on his space suit in his room, while the hostess explained how NASA had helped him get the protective suit. Then she closed the program, saying Jared had been filmed as part of Argentina's celebration of the Year of the Child.

The next day the TV crew left and Jared started school. The exuberance of the weekend died a quick death.

I went to the school, introduced myself to Jared's new teacher, pleasantly explained that Jared was on a home study program, and asked for his assignments and books. She said nonchalantly, "Oh, I haven't gotten them together yet. It'll take a while. We don't have any extra books for Jared."

I passed off her attitude to the fact that she was a very young woman, newly hired, fresh out of college and, perhaps, not familiar with how the school was conducting the home study program.

But when I got home and told Marlene what had happened, she went directly to the phone and called the principal, who oversaw the teacher's handling of Jared's home study program. "My husband was just in to pick up Jared's books and assignments, and the teacher didn't have anything ready for him. We're quite concerned about this. I was wondering how soon we will be able to pick them up."

"We don't have any books for Jared," the principal said curtly. "We'll have to order them from the publisher. That will take about six weeks."

"Six weeks? How could Jared catch up with the class after he's missed six weeks of school?"

"It doesn't matter. Jared's not an integrated student here anyway. He can finish school next summer during vacation."

"What do you mean, Jared's not an integrated student? He's been doing the same school work as his classmates, and we're paying the same tuition. It's not fair to expect Jared to do his school work during the summer when his brother and sister and friends in the neighborhood are home from school. Look, I don't understand. If all the other students get their books on the first day of school, why can't Jared?"

The principal did nothing to hide the sarcasm in

her voice. "Mrs. Reisman, the second-grade teacher has twenty other sweaty bodies to worry about. She doesn't have time to think about Jared."

Marlene turned to me, her face like ash, her voice barely audible.

"It's over. They're trying to expel Jared from school."

My first impulse was to find another school and just escape the viciousness of the situation. I phoned my supervisor at work and told him I wouldn't be in, then I opened the phone directory and spent the day calling private schools. Finding a new school, I found out quickly, would be just like our efforts to find a new doctor years before.

Every school I called said it would need to know Jared's academic standing, his current school, and our reasons for wanting to leave it. I knew no school would believe me if I told them Jared was an A student, but his school was expelling him. On the other hand, I couldn't go ahead and enroll Jared under false pretenses. The truth would come out soon enough, since a new school routinely requests the previous school's records before enrolling a student. Finally, even if I found another school that knew the whole "story" and accepted Jared anyway, Social Services would be there in no time flat.

We were locked into the current school. By the end of the day, I was madder than hell. Jared had his rights, and I was going to fight for them. Perhaps it would have been too much to expect them to resist outside pressures, but it seemed to me what the school was doing was illegal and immoral, so I decided to force its hand.

On the second day of school, I went to Jared's class just before the class was about to start. The teacher and several of the children were at the front of the room, discussing the day's projects. I could hardly hold my anger, looking at the children in their new school clothes, faces excited as they greeted old friends, compared lunch boxes, swapped stories about vacation. Why couldn't Jared have the simple pleasure millions of American children were enjoying—going to school? How could this teacher, seemingly so kind and human toward these children, be so cruel to Jared?

For Jared's sake, I had to control myself. "Excuse me," I said to the teacher politely. "Do you have any books or assignments for Jared?"

"No," she said with no perceptible emotion.

Marlene and Jared were waiting at home, depending on me to do something, and I couldn't bear the idea of going home empty-handed again. I had to think fast. "Can I borrow some of your books and duplicate a few pages?"

She was so surprised, she said yes. "Over there," and she pointed to a long table on the far side of the room stacked with textbooks, workbooks, and teachers' manuals.

I took a few books and went to the principal's office, where the secretary let me use the copy machine. I copied a few pages from each book, returned them to the classroom and drove home. Thus, Jared started second grade, in a manner of speaking.

I brought the school materials home, had a brief victory celebration with Marlene and Jared, and then went off to my job. That afternoon Marlene got a call from the vice-president of the company that supplied our house filters. She was really surprised. We had had regular communication with him for many months, but he'd always called me at work.

His first call to me had been to say that he'd seen Jared and Dr. Wilson on the NBC-TV program, "America Alive," where the company's filters were mentioned by name. He said the company was so delighted, it had bought the entire segment from NBC and planned to use it to advertise the filters. He'd had a long conversation with Dr. Wilson, who gave permission to use his name, and he was calling me now, he said, to get our permission so he could make up a sales brochure. Marlene and I gave it gladly. A few months later, he sent us the brochure, which used selected scenes and dialogue from the program and included a shot of Jared in his large bubble.

Another series of conversations I had with the vice-president stemmed from my mentioning how careful we had to be to keep the house doors and windows shut to prevent contamination from outside air. He was eager to help. "I can arrange to have a fresh air makeup system installed in your house. It'll keep the pressure inside higher than outside." Within a few weeks, the company had the system installed in our attic and even sent out two California representatives to check out the system. Marlene and I considered the filter company, and especially its vice-president, one of our staunchest supporters.

Now he was calling Marlene. He started the conversation by asking, "How is Jared doing in school?"

"He's doing just great. He's started second grade, and he got all A's on his report card last year.

"You mean he's not retarded?"

Marlene says she started to tremble and could hardly speak. She managed to mumble out, "Of course not."

"Well, I've just received a very upsetting letter from one of your doctors in Arizona, saying that Jared's case is a publicity hoax," and he named the physician.

"I've never heard of that doctor. I think the letter is a hoax."

"No, no, let me read the letter to you." In it, the alleged doctor said the air filters posed a threat to Jared's health and that both Jared and Marlene needed "psychiatric help." Marlene kept quiet.

"I've taken this matter up with our publicity department," the vice-president continued, "and we've decided, in view of the Arizona doctor's letter and other similar letters we've received from doctors, to discontinue the use of Jared in our ads."

"Fine," Marlene said abruptly and hung up the phone.

Marlene called me at work, and I could tell something was wrong as soon as she started talking. She repeated the conversation word for word. "Barry, doesn't it sound just like what happened with the safety equipment company? They hear from the doctors, then they want to stop the publicity?"

"Maybe, but I think something more is going on. How could his filters pose a threat to Jared's health? Why didn't he defend his own filters?"

"Remember when our air-conditioning contractor told us the filters are used in thousands of people's homes? Why isn't 'the Arizona doctor' concerned about the 'threat' to their health, too?"

I recalled the last time I'd bought filters. "The shop owner even told me they'd been installing the filters in medical buildings. The doctors in those buildings surely don't think the filters are harming their patients."

"Well, you know what I think?" Marlene said suddenly. "I think the vice-president knows the letter's a hoax. He's just using it as an excuse to tell us he's on the doctors' side and doesn't want his company associated with Jared's story. Maybe his legal department told him to notify us first, before he stopped the publicity, just in case."

I agreed with her, though there still were a lot of unanswered questions. We'd never asked the company for any favors; they'd always just offered to help us. We both assumed the matter had ended, that we'd lost the support of the filter company, that we'd lost another round. But this setback had one positive effect: I was determined, more than ever, to keep up the battle.

Now I wanted to force the school into some kind of action, so I showed up at Jared's class every morning to copy pages from his texts. After three weeks of this, the teacher asked to meet with Marlene and me. Of course, we expected the worst, that she was going to formally expel Jared. If this happened, at least we'd have the consolation of knowing the school would be forced to give a legitimate reason for its action. I then could argue our case and get some two-way communication started, based on Jared's right to get an education.

As we entered Jared's classroom, his teacher didn't even bother to say hello to us, withholding even this simple courtesy since there were no children in the room to overhear.

"Let us pray," were her opening words, head bowed. "Dear Lord, Mr. and Mrs. Reisman think they're doing right for Jared, but, Lord, you know what's right for him. Please help them so they'll do what's right for Jared. In Christ's name, amen."

I had come to expect almost anything from the school, but never this, a teacher hiding behind religion to sanction her actions. How could she have the audacity to tell God that what we'd done for Jared was against His will? Her prayer made it such that, to defend ourselves, we'd have to go against "God's will." I felt like screaming out, "Do you believe Jesus loves all the little children, except Jared? Is that why you can be so cruel to him?"

But we kept quiet. To her, we must have looked like a pair of unfeeling zombies. She grew bolder and finally spelled it out for us.

"Why don't you stop spinning your wheels and take Jared to Social Services? They'll take care of him for you."

I swallowed my gall and said firmly, trying to sound calm, "That's out of the question."

"I guess you don't like it because Social Services knows Jared's retarded."

We got up and left, but the meeting was not a waste. Now we had more evidence that Social Services was pressuring the school to expel Jared. In that respect, at least, we were probably more informed than Jared's young teacher, who didn't know Jared had gotten all A's in the first grade or that the school was using her, in all her ignorance, as a mouthpiece.

At home Marlene and I had one of our now all-too-familiar long strategy talks. "Why in the world would a school give in to Social Services and not defend its own student?" I wondered out loud.

"There's obviously nothing in it for the school to defend Jared. The principal's probably being pressured by some highly credentialed people—pillars of the community—and for all we know, some of our doctors or their associates are members of the church's congregation."

"Yes, and if the school staff helped us, they'd alienate a lot of their friends in the community. We're a real thorn in their side. They get rid of us, and their problems disappear."

Marlene was adamant. "Well, we're not going to disappear. Let's go back to the school and talk to the principal directly."

A few days later I worked up enough nerve to go see her. I just walked in, without an appointment. "May I have Jared's texts and assignments?"

"The press is on our side, you know," the principal said.

I stared at her. Inadvertently, she had as good as told me the school had been discussing Jared with the press. It gave me some insight into what probably had happened to touch off two curious events two months before.

Two newspapers and a magazine contacted us and asked to do an update on Jared's story, mainly, they said, to report on how he had fared in first grade. The reporters explained that his schooling was of special interest because of the previous retardation diagnosis.

When we told the reporters Jared had gotten all A's, they seemed very pleased and said they'd report it in their articles. They also asked for the name and phone number of Jared's school, so they could get a statement from the school staff, too. But, when the articles appeared, they contained updates on Jared's bubbles and space suit, and there wasn't a word about his schooling or his completing first grade with perfect grades. The omission surprised us, but we dismissed it, thinking the writers simply changed their minds or that their editors had to cut the articles for space reasons.

Another thing happened I didn't pick up on at the time. I had written a letter to the editor at a newspaper that had run several pieces on Jared. In my letter, I thanked the paper for the articles and told how Jared had successfully completed first grade, thinking the editor would be pleased with the follow-up information.

My letter never ran, and when I spoke with the editor later he told me why: "You'd have to change it before we'd be able to print it." I didn't really understand what he meant, but I didn't pursue it. Even when he asked me if any other newspapers had reported on Jared's schooling, I still didn't catch on. What was there to understand? Jared had finished first grade and I had his report card as proof. If the press was doubting that, why wouldn't they have asked me for the report card?

Everything came clear in the principal's office. The press had gotten its "first-hand" information from the school and probably from the principal herself, who told them what she had told us. Jared wasn't an integrated student. No wonder Jared's schooling wasn't mentioned in any of the articles. No wonder the principal thought the press was on her side.

I had to let her know that wasn't entirely true. "A TV crew just came up from Buenos Aires and did a '60 Minutes' documentary on Jared for the international celebration of the Year of the Child." She said nothing, just walked out of her office and returned a few minutes later carrying an armload of textbooks.

Walking to the car with the welcome burden of the books, it hit me. Apparently the documentary had saved Jared from expulsion.

But our problems with the school didn't disappear entirely. We got his assignments only every now and then. Some weeks Jared's teacher skipped them altogether, while on others she assigned him a double or triple workload. Marlene was careful to hand in Jared's completed assignments on time, but often she didn't get back the corrected and graded work for months. Despite the hardships under which Jared was studying, he did well in second grade and remained an A student.

During this school year, Jared was virtually ignored by his teacher. She never invited him to school to meet his classmates. At Christmastime, he didn't get an invitation to the class party or any greeting cards from his classmates. Fortunately, Jared didn't know he was being ignored by the school, at least not at first. He just accepted life as it was, and he was content to do his school work at home.

Then, shortly before Valentine's Day the teacher sent us a note telling us Jared would be exchanging cards with his classmates. She couldn't have picked a better holiday, for it was Jared's favorite. All his past treasures from the day—huge, lace-trimmed red hearts, cards, miniature candy hearts—became collector's items he displayed in his room.

With great excitement, he filled out the eighteen Valentine cards. The teacher had supplied a list of his classmates, and he learned their names for the first time. He knew many of the children from first grade, so writing the cards had a special, personal meaning for Jared. After he finished all his messages, he placed the cards neatly in a red heart-shaped folder he made himself. The day before Valentine's Day, I delivered the cards to the teacher.

Valentine's Day came and went. Jared got no cards or candies from the children. "Why didn't I get any cards?" he asked us over and over. "Did the kids get my cards?" "Did they like my cards?" "Don't they like me?" We tried to answer his questions obliquely at first, but we couldn't cover up. Jared caught on. He knew the school had played a trick on him.

And Marlene and I ourselves struggled to find a reason for the teacher's action against Jared. Our most charitable explanation was that she was trying to force us to withdraw him from the school, thereby sparing him from future suffering at their hands.

This vicious ruse affected Jared deeply, and he mentioned it often for weeks afterward. Then he'd cry and ask again, "Why didn't they give me any cards?" Sometimes, when this happened, we'd take him to a candy store to try to comfort him. It usually lifted his spirits a little. He had been terribly hurt, however, and would never forget what had been done to him.

One evening Marlene and I were watching a movie on TV. As children do, Jared was intermittently going in and out of the room. Then a scene caught his attention—a little boy had died, and during a lengthy funeral scene, the boy's classmates sang. Jared started sobbing, tears streaming down his face. "Daddy, when I die, then will the children come to see me?" What can you say to a little boy who thinks he would be abandoned even in death? We held him tightly and kissed him and tried to talk away his fears.

Despite these sad times, Jared was still basically a happy child. Marlene and I usually set aside Sundays for outings with the children. Often these started with my piling up our station wagon with David's golf clubs and an assortment of water and sand toys for Alicia and Jared. We'd drive to a golf course, drop off David for a day of golf, and go on to the American River, which flowed nearby. From its shores, Alicia and Jared waved to people floating by in their rubber rafts, waded in the water, built sand castles, sailed their little boats, and tried to catch the fish swimming by. Marlene and I would sit close to the water on beach chairs, keeping an eye on the children, relaxing and catching up on conversation lost during the busy week. Life seemed so right on those days. Jared and Alicia looked like any other children, spending a lazy day playing on the riverbank.

In late fall that year, we got a call from the producer of a nationally syndicated television show who wanted to do a segment on a typical day in Jared's life. We agreed to do the show.

Jared was all smiles when he opened the front door and saw the TV crew—host, producer, and cameraman with their lights, video camera, and cables. He watched intently as they slowly transformed our family room into a TV studio. As always, the filming went smoothly and everyone was in high spirits.

The crew was shooting Jared reading and doing math problems for the host, and I was standing behind the camera talking with the producer. As Jared started to read, I whispered casually that we were really proud of Jared's progress, that he had gotten all A's on his report card.

"Can I see the card?" the producer asked. I went to my desk and got it.

Without a word of explanation, the producer took the card and walked over to the cameraman. "Let's go into the other room. I want you to film this." From the other room, Marlene and I could overhear the producer telling the cameraman to film all sides of the card, including the teacher's signature.

"What's going on?" I asked when they finished.

The producer smiled. "It's an exposé."

At first I wasn't sure if he was kidding or not. Then, suddenly, I had the thought that the producer was being a little too secretive, that he might have thought we fabricated Jared's report card. I knew rumors were circulating in the community that Jared had been expelled from school, and I remembered what the newspaper editor had said to me months before. I had the horrible image of Jared's report card on TV, and the host of this program saying, off screen, that we'd made it up.

I tried to stay calm. "You can call the school and tell them you've seen Jared's report card if you like." The producer nodded affirmatively.

The school wouldn't deny the existence of the card, I was sure. In fact, at that moment, I was sorry I hadn't given the newspaper editor a copy of it. The rumors might have been stopped if I had.

The show aired a beautifully produced segment on Jared a few weeks later, but Jared's schooling and report card again weren't mentioned. We figured the producer either hadn't been able to corroborate the validity of the report card or, because it would have taken an investigation to get to the bottom of it, he'd decided to just drop it. It wasn't the kind of show that did investigative reporting.

11

Out of the Dark Ages

Not long after Jared's "typical day" was shot, yet another TV station called us. This time it was a Los Angeles station. The producer of its news department said she wanted to send a psychiatrist, who did a medical program for the station twice a week, to interview us and seven-year-old Jared. Marlene and I talked it over and decided it would be a good chance to have a doctor see all of us at home, see what was really going on here. We also felt that having Jared interviewed by a psychiatrist might help us with the school.

The psychiatrist, producer, and TV crew arrived at our house on the scheduled day and quickly set up their equipment. The psychiatrist exchanged perfunctory greetings with us but didn't discuss Jared or our story until the filming started.

The interview was hard-hitting, as if Mike Wallace were grilling us. The psychiatrist challenged every part of our story—Jared's illness, recovery, and treatment by the medical profession. Halfway through the interview he stopped the cameras, jumped up from his chair, and said, "My God! You've got to be telling the truth. No one could make up a story like that!"

The cameraman started shooting again. The interview continued, but the doctor's attitude had changed from hostility to sympathy. We named our doctors and talked some more. Then the interview with us was over.

The psychiatrist told us he'd do a complete investigation of the story. If he found we were lying, he'd put our doctors on TV and expose us. But if he could corroborate our story, he'd run the segment on Jared. However, he said, he wouldn't mention the way the doctors treated us. "As a doctor, I can't go against my fellow doctors," he explained.

"Doctor," Marlene said, "if we're wrong and you find Jared is severely retarded and autistic, we'll go on television with our doctors and apologize for what we've done. But I still want to be given credit for having changed a 'severely retarded boy,' who couldn't talk or walk, into a happy, active boy and a straight-A student."

"Jared was never brain-damaged," the doctor shot back. "That's not reversible!"

I glanced at Marlene. She gave me a big smile. Without her saying a word, I knew what she was thinking—how our pediatrician had told us to go to a psychiatrist, so we could accept Jared's retardation, and how she'd love to see the look on our pediatrician's face when this psychiatrist tells him he interviewed us.

Now the psychiatrist asked us to take him to a playground, so the crew could film Jared in his space suit playing with other children. We took them to the closest playground, at the public school, where the neighborhood children usually played after school. But, when we got there, the principal stormed out of his office and asked angrily, "What are you doing here?"

"This is a psychiatrist and his TV crew," I said calmly. "They want to film a short segment on Jared in the playground."

"I don't want any part of this. You have no right to be here!"

For a few moments I felt like I was having an out-of-body experience, looking down on the pained expressions of the doctor, producer, and cameraman, all standing there speechless, like they didn't know what hit them.

As we left the playground, I told the psychiatrist we'd had similar episodes before.

"What's happening to you is like something out of the Dark Ages," he said in disbelief. "No one should have to live like this."

He still wanted some footage of Jared playing

with other children, so we went to our neighborhood park. There the crew filmed him playing and talking with other youngsters, as the psychiatrist watched intently. "Look how well he relates," he said excitedly to the producer. "He's not autistic."

We came home, and they filmed Jared reading from his textbook and doing math. On his own, the psychiatrist brought up the subject of Social Services. "Right now, the law assumes that Social Services knows more about taking care of handicapped children than parents do. I don't agree with that." They were beautiful words I thought I'd never hear from a doctor.

At the end of the day, the doctor climbed into Jared's bubble isolator to interview him. We saw immediately that he had a real professional knack for putting patients at ease. He got Jared in a talkative mood by asking about the toys in his bubble, one of which was a set of plastic numbers. The doctor started holding up two numbers at a time and asking Jared for their sum.

"Five plus four equals what, Jared?"

"Nine," Jared said immediately.

Jared got all the sums right. Then he began holding up numbers for the doctor to add, giggling with delight as he watched the doctor pause dramatically to think and then come up with the right answer. Finally the doctor held up two more numbers. "This is a real hard one, Jared. What does one plus one equal?"

"Poop," Jared answered, rolling over laughing at the joke he'd played on the doctor.

After the interview, the psychiatrist told us, "Jared's a beautiful and intelligent child."

The research department of the Los Angeles TV station called us three months later to tell us they'd finished investigating the story and would be doing two segments on Jared. The researcher said, "The psychiatrist asked me to tell you that what the doctors did to you will not be mentioned."

So Marlene and I knew two things: Our story had checked out, and the psychiatrist, though he now knew the truth, would not go against our doctors publicly.

During the week the TV segments on Jared ran, I got a call at work from the vice-president of the filter company, who said he was phoning from Los Angeles. I was surprised to hear from him again. We'd had no communication with him for months, ever since he'd made it clear to Marlene that company publicity using Jared would be stopped. Now what did he want?

"Barry, I need your help," he said, sounding frantic. "We placed Jared's ad in a medical journal, and I just got a disturbing letter from the journal's publisher. I'm taking it up with my legal department."

"What journal did you place it in?"

"It's an allergy journal."

"Look, you told us last fall you wouldn't be doing any more ads. I'd like to see this one. Could you send me a copy?"

"Well, uh, I have it right here. It has some flowers on the cover. It's pretty big. It wouldn't be convenient to send."

I had no doubts that some intrigue was going on, but I didn't tell him how ridiculous it all sounded. I just listened, trying to figure out what was happening, hoping that, if I stayed calm, he might inadvertently let the cat out of the bag.

"So, how can I help you?" I asked.

"The journal publisher said he'd received a lot of letters from doctors saying Jared's story is a hoax. One was a doctor who examined Jared in Denver, who said Jared didn't need filters and was retarded. Could you please phone the journal's publisher and give him some proof that Jared really needs the filters?"

"What kind of proof does he want?"

"All he really needs is proof that Jared went to the Mayo Clinic. Do you have any correspondence or medical records from them that you could send the publisher?"

"I'll look into it," I said coolly. The call was starting to make a little more sense. It looked like the Denver doctors had asked the vice-president and the journal publisher to get hold of any Mayo Clinic records or correspondence we had. From NJH's point of view, the records of the immunology test Mayo ran could point up how ludicrous NJH's treatment of Jared had been. We assumed the NJH doctors feared the Mayo Clinic records could be used against them.

"A psychiatrist investigated our story, and he interviewed Jared for a TV program," I told the vice-president. "He found Jared to be an intelligent child. In fact, the last segment of what he filmed will be on TV in L.A. tomorrow night. Since you're there, why don't you watch it?"

The vice-president didn't say a word. His silence made it clear to me that he wasn't interested in whether our story was the "hoax" the doctors said it was. He was interested only in getting some "help" from us. But why?

He ended our conversation by giving me the publisher's address and asking me to send any medical records I had. Then, a few days later he sent me a copy of the "letter" he'd received from the publisher. In part, it read:

> In regard to the previous advertisement, we received a letter from a clinical allergist who read the August advertisement and wrote us a letter that contained the following:
>
> "I am writing this letter to you in an attempt to express displeasure over an advertisement in the journal. I realize the value and importance of these advertisements to the maintenance and well-being of a publication, but I think that as responsible physicians we have to exercise some care in what is allowed. There appeared in your August issue an advertisement for air cleaners. In the advertisement a case was presented of a certain young man named Jared Reisman.
>
> "This is the same Jared Reisman who came to Denver and whose family managed to obtain for him and themselves a great deal of newspaper publicity and theatrical displays. It has never been established that Jared has significant allergic disease or that he needs any of the filtration devices for the disease from which he 'suffers.' We here have an unfortunate example, I believe, of a family exploiting a potential illness in their child. It is clear from the physicians who worked with him at National Jewish Hospital

that Jared was not a normal child. I can see no justification for the inclusion of his case history and name and a picture of him in a bubble other than the cheapest of advertising devices showing the most superficial concern about patient welfare. I believe it would be in the best interest of the Academy and what it stands for to ask this company to remove that particular advertisement from general medical journals and journals such as ours."

We had several reactions to the letter. First, we didn't believe it. We felt it had been fabricated and wondered if the publisher and the vice-president were players in the game. We also were appalled by the unjust indictment of Jared and the outright lies in the letter from the "clinical allergist."

We didn't write back to the vice-president, and we didn't try to defend ourselves with the publisher. We weren't going to deal with people who were trying to destroy Jared. But for weeks afterward, Marlene and I had long discussions, trying to piece together why the filter company was getting so involved in our lives and what it was trying to do.

There were so many unknowns. How long had the vice-president been involved in helping the doctors stop publicity about Jared? Before the company bought the NBC "America Alive" segment on Jared and Dr. Wilson and asked our permission to use portions of it in its sales brochure? After that, but sometime before the vice-president called Marlene, told her of the "complaints" about the publicity, and said Jared's ads would be discontinued? Was he actually part of a conspiracy? The timing seemed critical if we were to make sense out of his motives in asking for our "help" now.

Then there was the question of whether the vice-president really believed that the doctors' retardation diagnosis was right. Could he have believed that Jared didn't need his filters? If he had any doubts, why didn't he check with Dr. Wilson, whom he knew?

And, finally, why had he recently run an ad with Jared in it in the allergy journal, the one "with some flowers on the cover" that he clearly didn't want us to see? Did the ad even exist, or was it, too, part of a fabrication?

We had our theory: Early on, the vice-president had been convinced either that the retardation diagnosis was correct or simply that continued publicity using Jared, a controversial subject, would be damaging to the company's reputation. Regardless of which scenario was true, it appeared to us that the vice-president decided, perhaps at the urging of the company's legal department, to stop the advertising with Jared in it and use the complaining letters as the reason.

It seemed to us that the medical community must have been delighted to have the support of the filter company. They'd get the publicity stopped, and they'd have a new, powerful weapon to use against us in the press—the filter company didn't believe our story, either.

But something had gone wrong. We guessed that the latest ad, real or not, and the vice-president's cry for help were an attempt to get the company out of a legal bind. Who knows? Maybe someone, we don't know who, was threatening the company with some legal action, something to do with us and the company's role in Jared's story. Maybe someone had told the vice-president legal action would be dropped if he would help get the critical Mayo Clinic records. We had to stretch our imaginations to entertain such unbelievable ideas, but after all our years of fighting, nothing seemed farfetched.

A few months later our theory about the vice-president was pretty well borne out. Marlene got a call from him. She felt like slamming down the phone as soon as he identified himself, but, fortunately, she decided to play along to see what he was up to. He explained that the company was having an annual sales conference, and he was calling to ask her to make a videotaped statement that would be filmed by a local TV station. Marlene could hardly believe he was asking her to do this, but she stayed calm and didn't commit herself one way or the other. The vice-president said he'd send her the script.

The script arrived by Mail-a-Gram the next day. It called for Marlene to say how beneficial the filters had been for Jared and to thank the company. But in the middle of the script lay the real motive for the tape: Marlene was supposed to say, "In all our dealings with the company, it has been fair and honest, but more important, it has helped Jared enjoy life." We had to laugh. After all they'd done, they now expected us to go on record saying they were fair and honest. We didn't even answer the Mail-a-Gram.

Then, a few days later, Marlene got a call from a woman at a local TV station. She said she'd be producing the videotape "for the firm back East," and she asked to set up an appointment to come to our house.

"We won't be doing the tape for the filter company," Marlene said.

"I haven't heard from any filter company," the woman said, sounding surprised. "I've been talking with an attorney from a public relations firm, and he's the one who wants the tape. He just told me it's very important, and that if I couldn't reach you by phone, I was supposed to come out to your house."

Marlene apologized, said there'd be no tape, and hung up.

The woman didn't know it, but she had let us know how desperately the company wanted the tape. It appeared that the company wanted to protect itself by using our taped testimonial as evidence that it wasn't guilty of any wrongdoing.

We never heard from the company again. But a year later, it ran a full-page ad of Jared in *TV Guide* magazine. We felt vindicated: It was the company's way of saying publicly, on record, that it hadn't gone against Jared.

12

Still on the Books: Retardation

Jared today is a tall, energetic twelve-year-old. He's in the sixth grade and continues to do well in school, learning quickly and excelling in math and science. Right now he says he'd like to be an astronomer when he grows up.

But, like an alien, Jared is still peering at the world through his bubbles, unable to breathe our air without protection, the air that most of us take for granted. We hope someday he'll outgrow his illness or a cure will be found, so he can study to be an astronomer or anything else he wants to be.

Jared hasn't been in a classroom since those few weeks in first grade. He's still on the home study program. Every weekday he does the same assignments his classmates are doing. Once a week I go to his school, pick up his assignments, and hand in his completed work. No teacher has ever invited Jared to class since the first grade, and no teacher has ever asked about him when I've met with them. To them, Jared is a nonentity, an oddity of our community to be tolerated but never acknowledged.

We still are profoundly disappointed that the medical system we believed in didn't work for Jared. We had started out with complete trust in the system, and that's why, during the years of Jared's illness, we pleaded with the doctors for help rather than arguing with them. Not once did we have even a minor argument or exchange harsh words with a physician. Somehow we always believed we'd get good medical care eventually.

To this day we can hardly believe what's been done to Jared. We don't know why the original medical error snowballed into a hostile community reaction. But we're trying to deal with it coolly, without hostility, hoping that somehow our attitude will affect those who have tried to undermine our efforts to keep Jared alive, and that rationality and calmness will prevail.

He has been hurt deeply by his forced separation from other children and often asks, "When can I go to school and have friends?" Marlene and I try to assure him that someday his illness might end, and he'll be able to go to school with other kids.

In the meantime, he's excited about the prospect of becoming a teenager, maybe attending high school, learning to drive a car. "Grade school's for little kids anyway," he says sometimes. His new interest in "growing up" has created a new bond between him and David. Jared's impressed by David's great age—seventeen—his high school stories, and his driving lessons. They have boy-to-boy talks about cars, crime, the draft, girls.

David is still doing very well in school, and, as always, we're proud of him. He graduated from junior high at the top of his class and scored so high on the SAT tests, he was eligible to take college entrance exams, which he did well on, too. He's a member of the school math club and golf team.

Alicia's now in the third grade at the neighborhood public school. Every afternoon, Marlene takes Jared along to pick up Alicia, who runs to the car, all excited, ready to share her day with him. "Look, Jared, look what I made today," she says, and together they look over her artwork, papers, and library books.

Like most kids their age, Jared and Alicia are hooked on computers. They spend almost every evening playing games on the Atari. Jared's something of a whiz kid at these games. He's so good at them and so intent, sometimes it's hard to get him away from the board. He's called me at work to ask for a new game, and once he called just to say, "Dad, I don't think I was really happy until I got my computer!"

And Marlene and I? Well, in spite of everything that's happened, we feel lucky to have made it this far. We continue to have our marathon talks about

the events of the past few years and why a community would go against a little boy. But we'll always be
greatly indebted to the people along the way who
stepped in to help Jared, including the press for telling our story. We still have faith in mankind. I know
there are a lot of good people out there.

Most of Jared's equipment, and much of it that
we still use today, was donated—the fresh air
makeup system for our home, the commercial model
home air purifier, the helmet and respirator from
Bruce Held, the air purifier for motel and car use, the
plastic bubble isolators, the clear plastic head bubble. Of course, Dr. Wilson generously donated his
time when he visited us and when he designed and
coordinated the manufacture of the bubbles.

The mainstay of Jared's continued health are the
house filters, which give him complete freedom indoors without the need for a face mask, and his head
bubble and backpack respirator, which he wears
when he goes outside.

About three years ago I replaced Jared's hard hat
helmet with a lightweight clear plastic head bubble
that I purchased "over the counter" from a safety
equipment company. I had to modify the inlet hose
ducting so I could attach the old hose securely to the
back of the head bubble. As before, the same motorized blower supplies filtered air to the bubble. The
new head bubble has the advantages of better visibility, lighter weight, ready availability from a commercial supplier, and size—it's an adult size so Jared
won't outgrow it.

Marlene and I continue to search for new and
improved equipment for Jared. We just ordered a

quieter portable respirator that runs eight hours on a battery charge and uses a small rubberized face mask. Recently introduced by a safety equipment company, the new face mask should be less confining and allow Jared to hear better. We're also hoping for an even greater benefit. If Jared is someday accepted in the community, he might be able to use the new respirator at school because the battery lasts longer and it's quieter.

Despite Jared's absence of symptoms and outwardly robust appearance, we still have to vigilantly maintain superclean surroundings for him. Filtered air alone doesn't assure his safety. Good housekeeping is essential. Saturday and Sunday mornings we vacuum carpets, furniture, and walls, and clean windows. Marlene hand-scrubs the floors several times a week, making sure no dust remains.

Marlene can get quite drained from some of these labors, especially during weeks when Jared's assignments, and thus her teaching loads, are heavy. It amazes me how she keeps up the routine. Once I tried hand-scrubbing the floors, but I was completely spent in an hour. So I went out and bought some professional cleaning equipment—a pail with a wringer and heavy-duty mop—determined to do the job in a more "civilized" manner. But the modern method was too coarse and didn't get up all the dust. Marlene continues with the hand method.

Our house filters work only if the furnace blower is on, pumping filtered air through floor ducts in each room. We run the blower twenty-four hours a day, keep all windows closed, and scrupulously keep to a minimum the times we open outside doors to cut down on infiltration of airborne allergens. Unfortunately, the efficiency of the supplementary attic filters was dropping to too low a level during the high allergy seasons. We had to disconnect the fresh air makeup system we'd installed years ago to create a positive pressure in the house. That means that standing by an open front door, casually talking with a visitor, is a luxury we can't afford. So is trying to catch a cool evening breeze at an open window after a hot summer day.

Spring and summer are particularly high aeroallergen seasons, and we're especially careful then. After I mow the lawn, for example, I enter the house through a side door that leads into the utility room, which is closed off from the rest of the house. There I strip off my clothes and throw them in the washing machine. Then, after a quick shower and shampoo, I can join the family again. Without going through that process, I would bring in irritants on my clothing and hair.

In order to keep up my heavy job schedule and home chores, I try to stay in top physical shape. For years I've gone to a local gym three times a week to lift weights, jog, and swim. I find it helps keep up my spirits as well as my energy level. Who knows? Someday I may even be able to hand-scrub floors.

As for Dr. Wilson, after our trip to the National Jewish Hospital, we received a long letter from him describing a lengthy conversation he'd had with the doctors there and his attempt to explain to them Jared's illness and need for the bubbles. The whole episode at Denver, Dr. Wilson said, resulted from some unfortunate misunderstandings among the doctors. He had been able to contact a hospital in Los Angeles, however, and was hoping they could investigate Jared's complex case. We never heard from him on this matter again. We can only assume that even he was helpless in getting care for Jared.

Over the years, we've exchanged holiday greetings with him. He invited us to his formal inauguration as president of the University of Portland.

Despite our disappointment, Marlene and I were greatly pleased by information in another of Dr. Wilson's letters to us. He said some good was coming from the publicity given to Jared's case. He said he'd received many inquiries from people suffering from aeroallergens, and to help them he was drawing up a standard information sheet with the specifications for our house filters and the filtering system for our bubbles. Over the years, the knowledge that others may have been helped has reduced some of our feelings of helplessness. If just one person was spared the suffering Jared endured, our efforts were well worth it.

We're still using the bubble isolators Dr. Wilson designed. Without these bubbles, Jared wouldn't be able to go on vacations and visit other states. And Jared knows this. It's meant a lot to him. One place he really needed and used his bubbles was on our trip to Durango, Colorado, in the summer of 1983.

Despite the heavily wooded area, Jared slept comfortably at night and romped by day at the nearby Mesa Verde National Park, site of the cliff dwellings of the prehistoric Mesa Verde Indians. Looking and feeling fit in his head bubble and back pack, he rambunctiously climbed down the mountainside on the steep ladders that lead to the cliff dwellings of this ancient civilization. Here was our boy, looking like an astronaut in his space-age gear, running and playing among the ancient Indian ruins. As he stood on the mesa, looking up wide-eyed at the Rocky Mountains, Jared captured the feeling one gets at Mesa Verde: "I think this is the most beautiful place I'll ever see in my life."

Our family life has more or less returned to normal, except for the long hours Marlene must spend tutoring Jared on the home study program and the cleaning involved to maintain a dust-free environment. Jared's illness is a thing of the past. He's been free of his symptoms for years in our air-filtered home. And Marlene and I have been able to spend more time together as a couple, making up for lost time.

We believe to this day that our local doctors and the doctors at National Jewish Hospital thought we couldn't distinguish between retardation and normal, even exceptional intelligence. However, with two other children, we had firsthand experience with normal, early-childhood development. They treated us as if Jared was our only child, as if we lacked any yardstick with which to judge him.

Jared's misdiagnosis is still on the books. As far as we know, our local doctors have not changed their retardation diagnosis. Nor have any of them contacted us to inquire about Jared.

We've always known that we weren't alone, that, like Jared, many children have been misdiagnosed. One night about a year ago, I'd just fallen asleep when Marlene came running into the bedroom:

"Wake up, Barry! There's a program on '20/20' on the misdiagnosis of deaf children."

The word "misdiagnosis" was enough to startle me out of a sound sleep. We watched the show intently. For the first time, we learned how shamefully prevalent is the misdiagnosis of deaf children. A professor from Western Maryland College said one-third of the 2 million deaf Americans were diagnosed incorrectly when they were children. Even with our current, sophisticated medical knowledge, each year several thousand deaf children are being misdiagnosed as retarded, autistic, schizophrenic, brain-damaged, or a combination of these. The misdiagnoses, the professor said, are being made by experts who should know better. Worse, these diagnoses often are made in a few minutes. The tragedy is not only the loss of proper education during the critical early years, but also the second-class existence to which these children are relegated—permanently.

The host interviewed the parents of a deaf girl who, as a young child, was incorrectly diagnosed as schizophrenic after a five-minute examination. Improperly treated as emotionally disturbed, she soon did develop emotional problems. And when her deafness finally was discovered, she couldn't leave her problems behind. After years spent around disturbed children, she, of course, behaved as they did.

The girl's parents have a lawsuit pending against many of the doctors who treated their daughter and the schools that "educated" her. In the court papers, the doctors and schools vigorously deny the charges of improper treatment, maintaining that the girl had emotional problems to begin with. But the parents don't see it that way. As Marlene and I listened to the story unfold, there was no question of who we sided with. The same thing would have happened to Jared if we'd allowed the doctors to put him into a school for the retarded. He soon would have acted truly retarded.

The girl's parents were asked why they hadn't acted sooner if they felt their daughter wasn't disturbed. Their answer spoke for all parents who want to do what's "right" for their children and whose gut feelings run counter to medical advice. As they went from doctor to doctor, they said, they felt trapped by their own ignorance. The medical professionals said their daughter was disturbed, and the "right" thing to do was to accept that fact.

Later in the interview, the mother said that not being able to function as a mother, not being able to nurture her daughter, was the biggest hurt. Marlene and I knew the feeling all too well, and just reliving it filled us with rage. There's no greater pain, no more devastating guilt, than being forced to give up on your own child when you believe there's still hope. I don't think it's something any parent can fully recover from.

13   *"This Big Guy"*

Jared started probing us in earnest about his illness two years ago—why he couldn't go outside without his bubble, how his bubbles worked, what was going on in his body. Marlene, always sensitive to the most positive ways to get through to Jared, explained that he probably had an overactive immune system, that the white cells—the "fighters" in his blood—were too good and were overreacting to particles in the air like pollen, dust, and mold. She said his white cells were like tiny, brave warriors, waging such a terrific battle against those particles that sometimes they made his body release substances that made him sick. But, at other times, these cells helped to keep him well by fighting off cold and flu germs.

Jared was intrigued by the explanation: "Isn't it better to have an overactive immune system than one that doesn't work good?" he asked. "I can really do a good job of fighting bad germs."

In some ways, Jared was right. He has been able to fight off the few colds and flus he's had since we installed the house filters. These common illnesses were mild, and none of his old symptoms flared up. Luckily, he was vaccinated before he was eighteen months old, before his illness began, and he had no allergic reaction to it.

Looking at Jared in our house, free of the symptoms, it's hard to imagine he was ever sick. A visitor would never guess that his life depends on the filtered air around him. He romps through the house like any normal, lively twelve-year-old.

Still, Jared knows he's dependent on the filters. He senses when they're not working properly and tells me when they have to be changed. He's always right. When I do change them—about every four months—they're always filled with dust. Marlene and I may not see any allergy symptoms, but Jared knows the headaches and tiredness he feels mean he's getting sick. He feels better as soon as I put in new filters.

Though Jared's life depends on those filters, Marlene makes a special effort to keep him from becoming psychologically dependent on them. She reminds him that someday he'll probably outgrow his allergies. "If you ever feel you can go outside without your bubble, Jared, go to the door and try it out," she tells him often.

Whenever he senses the time is right, especially during spring rainstorms, he ventures out. In the backyard, arms outstretched, head thrown back, he stands in ecstasy while the rain falls on his face. Then he dashes madly around the yard, jumping and skipping, and after a few minutes he darts back into the house, dripping wet and grinning. We keep encouraging his excursions and are confident that someday he'll walk to the front door and set himself free.

We know we've been fortunate to have Jared in such excellent health. And we know he'd be in serious trouble if he ever needed emergency surgery, for example, since he couldn't tolerate drugs or anesthetics. For that reason, we've always hoped the root causes of Jared's illness could be pinpointed and then a class of medications found that he could tolerate, at least in emergencies.

So we've kept searching for medical care for Jared. We've written several prominent medical clinics noted for their work in immunology, giving them Jared's medical history, and the results of his examination at the Mayo Clinic. Most didn't even answer, probably because we didn't have a local doctor's referral. Or perhaps they did phone one or more of our local doctors—our letters mentioned the medical centers where Jared had had hearing and allergy tests—and ran up against the retardation diagnosis. Even so, it seems odd to us that none of the clinics would see Jared, even for a preliminary exam.

We considered going back to the Mayo Clinic, especially since they had been so receptive to Jared's problem, but we decided not to risk it after what had happened in Denver. We feared that whoever had contacted NJH about the retardation diagnosis might also contact the Mayo Clinic. Also, Dr. Wilson had told us there were only a few medical centers with the special diagnostic tools to detect Jared's type of immunological and metabolic disorder, and the Mayo Clinic was not on his list.

One doctor at an eastern hospital did write back, but only to say she had talked with her hospital's pediatric hematologist, a "very knowledgeable person" who, unfortunately, "had no ideas to contribute," and with the chief of immunology, a doctor whose reputation was "top notch," who also had no significant recommendations. She referred us to a University of California medical school.

We didn't write to them because even before our trip to the National Jewish Hospital, Dr. Wilson had checked out appropriate immunology departments in the university system and couldn't find any doctor who would investigate Jared's problem.

Fortunately, Jared has needed emergency care only once. The summer he was nine, we took the children on a short vacation to Santa Cruz, an ocean resort area south of San Francisco noted for its boardwalk and amusement park. Jared, of course, was thrilled by his first roller coaster and Ferris wheel rides. We ended one of our days there with the sky glider, a slow-moving, 1,000-foot-long tram ride, the length of the boardwalk.

Alicia and I took the first car, and Marlene and

Jared got into the car behind us. The young attendant quickly pulled down their handlebar, and off the car went—with the handlebar locked in place on Jared's hand. The attendant never heard Marlene's shouts for help, but I did. Looking back I saw Jared's pained face and heard Marlene's futile screams. I started yelling for help, too, but we were sixty feet over the park, and no one could hear us.

Marlene tried desperately to free Jared's hand as I watched, terrified. I was certain that if she pulled on the handlebar too suddenly, she and Jared would plunge to their death. I was drenched in sweat. The ride seemed to take an eternity. Finally, at the end of the line, a shaken-looking attendant released Jared's hand. It looked squashed and had ugly, deep machinery imprints on it, and it started to swell immediately.

At the park's emergency treatment room, a nurse examined Jared's hand carefully. I was terrified watching Jared and wondering what the nurse and the doctor standing nearby were thinking. What would we do if they refused to treat Jared?

The nurse asked Jared why he was wearing a bubble, and he answered, matter-of-factly, "I've got bad allergies." And that's all there was to that. The nurse nodded and kept chatting amiably with Jared, then told us there were no broken bones. She gave us an ice pack to use until the swelling went down.

When the ordeal was over, Marlene and I felt almost giddy with relief over Jared's relatively minor injury and, more important, about the fact that he had been treated like any other patient. We were lucky this time, and we knew it. It reminded us of the paranoia we'd lived with for many years. It recon-firmed our need to continue searching for help for Jared.

But, as we search, Jared plows ahead, trying to grow up as normally as possible. He's always fought his isolation head on. A real live wire, he's very talk-ative and makes his presence known in the house-hold. He and Marlene are close, since they spend so much time in the house together. During the week-day evenings, however, Jared makes his rounds, making sure he also spends time with the rest of us. Usually he starts with Alicia, then goes on to David for, say, a board game, and winds up in the den spending the rest of the evening with me, watching TV and talking over the day's events.

With three growing children, our house is cer-tainly not all sweetness and roses. Jared, David, and Alicia have their arguments. And, like any normal little boy, there are times Jared won't listen to us when we reprimand him. But when Jared gets into a fight with someone he often phones Grandma. Then it's up to her to referee what Jared calls the family commotion, and he usually listens when she hands down her verdict.

Besides settling arguments, Grandma is also Jared's closest confidante. In his daily calls to her, along with their talks about his latest interests or something he's seen on the news or read in a lesson, he'll tell her things he won't discuss with us. She's not only his loving Grandma, she's also another con-nection to the outside, another way for Jared to fight isolation. Marlene and I are grateful for their mar-velous rapport.

During the school term, Jared fills his days with studying. He gets up early every morning and takes a long, leisurely shower, followed by a quick breakfast. Then, at 9:30 sharp, he goes to Marlene's room, ready for the day's assignments. It amazes Marlene that he voluntarily and happily keeps up this routine, right on schedule.

Jared likes to start the day sitting next to Marlene while she explains the assignments. Then he goes and works alone at the kitchen table, occasionally checking back with Marlene, making sure he's doing the lesson right. Marlene's particular, and Jared knows she expects a lot from him.

Science and social studies lessons are Jared's favorites, and he can talk these subjects into the ground. Often he climbs into bed at night with his dictionary, encyclopedia, and atlas to look up moonrise or moonset times, or how bacteria make yogurt, or whatever has grabbed his attention from the day's lessons.

Jared seems to truly enjoy his home study program, never rebels against doing school work and has admirable study habits, all of which Marlene attributes to the John Tracy Clinic course work he took when he was four and five years old. He used to spend long hours every day with Marlene then, learning to speak, read, and do arithmetic, so when he started home study work, it seemed a natural extension of the Tracy course.

As serious as Jared is about his studies, he's still a fun-loving boy. Because he's so often homebound, he's thrilled by certain experiences other kids his age may take somewhat for granted. Christmas, for example, has always been a time of great excitement for him. He loves to look out his window at the neighbors' outdoor lighting and the decorated trees in their windows, but best of all is the nighttime tour of Sacramento we take right before Christmas. From inside his car bubble in the back seat of the car, he ooh's and ah's over every elaborately decorated home—lights, trees, nativity displays. I think more than presents, the family tour is the high point of Christmas for him.

Then there's Halloween, the one day of the year Jared can go out looking like every other kid. When he first got his protective suit and I took him trick-or-treating around the neighborhood, he'd positively glow when another kid or adult asked where he got his neat space suit. Lately he gets a real kick out of wearing his bubble and space-motif Halloween costume to hand out candy at the front door. He will spend a long time talking and answering questions, especially from older kids, about his unique "costume."

And then there are the movies. Just after Jared turned ten, he got to see his first film in a theater. He'd always wanted to see a "real" movie, and when *Return of the Jedi* came out, he begged me to figure out a way he could go see it. I made some adjustments on his respirator so he could hear better, and the children and I went off to the movies.

Everything was so new to Jared—standing in line, buying tickets, sitting in the dark theater, eating popcorn by loosening the drawstring on his head bubble and feeding himself through the opening. The positive pressure of excess filtered air inside the head bubble prevents dirty outside air from leaking in. He sat totally engrossed throughout the movie, almost spellbound by the big screen. When it was over, all he could say for a while was, "That's real magic." And I felt fantastic—Jared had just enjoyed another normal childhood experience.

Jared thrives on these seemingly ordinary events. He grows with every one of them. But he also survives on inspiration he finds around him. Last year he read the biography of Theodore Roosevelt, who had severe asthma as a child, but grew up healthy because his father took him to live in the mountains. Jared got very excited by the similarities between Roosevelt's childhood disability and his own. "Mom," he shouted out one evening, "Roosevelt was a bubble boy, too!" By the time Jared got to the end of the story and learned that Roosevelt not only recovered completely but also went on to become president, he was as ecstatic as we've ever seen him.

That book held another source of inspiration. Jared learned that Roosevelt's father, who strongly believed that exercise would help his son overcome his asthma, made Roosevelt follow a daily regimen. At Jared's urging, we bought him an exercise bike and workout bench. He took to the bike like a duck to water. The first day he pedaled ten miles, and he's been pedaling furiously ever since. His cheerful efforts to make himself better, stronger, help us keep our hopes up, too.

And we have other reasons for hope. Marlene and I will never forget what Dr. Wilson said after he first visited us. We were at the airport, and as he put his arm around Marlene, he warmly and reassuringly told us he felt Jared someday would outgrow his illness—that, since the filters were keeping the illness under control, Jared's body would have a good chance of healing itself. Coming from a prominent immunologist, those words of encouragement have kept us going over the years.

As Marlene and I watch Jared grow in so many ways, we see that he, too, is starting to realize he's growing up and leaving his little-boy days behind. Since he turned twelve, one of his favorite TV shows is "Charlie's Angels." One night he came over to me and asked, "Where do you find beautiful girls like that? I'd sure like to find a girl who looks like one of Charlie's Angels!"

Then, just a few weeks ago, as Marlene and I were getting ready for bed, Jared stopped us and said mischievously, "I want to give you a good-night kiss."

"Jared, don't act silly," Marlene said, mock-sternly.

He ignored her remark and hugged us both, planting big, smooching kisses on our cheeks. As he left our room, walking out in elaborately casual, almost adolescent-looking strides, he laughed over his shoulder, and said, "You'd better appreciate that. This big guy may never kiss you again."

14   *The Haven*

Over the years of Jared's illness, I'd always wondered if there was any place on earth where he could live and breathe the air like anyone else. Several allergists had mentioned that the ideal environment for an allergy patient was a high-altitude area with a dry-desert climate, but none knew of such a haven. They said, as far as they knew, where these places once had existed, now they'd been spoiled by pollution and the planting of trees and grass.

When Jared was almost ten, I decided to find out

if that environment still existed anywhere. I enlisted the help of a colleague, a meteorologist. I knew if anyone could come up with the answer, he could. The man's a walking encyclopedia, and there's no problem too difficult for him to tackle. I told him I was looking for a place that was high, dry, and low in pollen and mold. "I'll find it for you, Barry," he said, over the stacks of books in his cluttered office.

A few days later he called me over. "Well, I think Albuquerque, New Mexico, is the best place." He opened several reference books and showed me charts on the city's altitude, rainfall, pollen count. The figures were impressive. No other area fit the allergists' criteria better.

I called Marlene and gave her the promising news. We'd decided earlier that, if my colleague found a place that fit the bill, we'd take a family trip there during our upcoming vacation. I made the arrangements that same day. We were a two-hour plane ride away from knowing if our haven existed.

When we arrived at the airport security checkpoint before our flight, two guards rushed out and started frisking Jared. Frightened speechless, he held up his arms rigidly as the guards checked his helmet and backpack. The tenseness of the situation broke when one guard started laughing. "Oh, I know what this is. Firemen use this safety equipment. Sorry, folks. You can go through."

"Are they going to arrest me?" Jared asked, still frozen in position.

We reassured him that everything was okay. It was an eventful start for Jared's first flight.

Jared sat awestruck, looking out the window as

the engines roared, and the plane picked up speed on the runway and lifted off. Once we were up in the clouds, he relaxed, then broke out laughing. "I feel like I'm taking a trip to heaven. It's so beautiful out there, I wish I could get out and run and play on the clouds!"

In Albuquerque we rented a car and drove through the city to our motel. The children oohed and aahed at the city's colorful beauty and Spanish architecture. Everyone was in high spirits as we drove up to the motel.

We hadn't been there more than a few minutes when David and Alicia started pleading in unison to go swimming in the pool. Tomorrow, I promised. Marlene and I kept looking over at Jared, waiting to see if he noticed any difference in the air. We'd decided not to tell him he might feel better here. We wanted him to notice the difference, if there was any, himself.

It happened the next day. We were in our rooms and Jared said casually, "The air feels good here, better than Sacramento. Is it cleaner here?"

"Yes," I said, smiling. "There's supposed to be less pollen and mold here. How would you like to try going outside?"

"I want to go in the pool. Can I wear the little mask?" He had a new, nonmotorized, half-face mask respirator with built-in filtering cartridges, a commercially available product we bought for the occasion. We had told him he might be able to wear it here.

I gave him the go-ahead. He got into his swimming trunks in what seemed like a split second. Then

I put the small respirator on him, fastened the elastic headbands, and we all went outside. Jared stood perfectly still, his eyes sparkling, looking happily at the surroundings, his eyes, ears, forehead, and hair free to the air and sun. Without the noise and confinement of his helmet and motorized respirator, he could hear the sounds of our world, and they surprised him. "It's noisy out here," he said. "I can hear birds singing."

At the pool, Jared stepped cautiously into the water. It was such a little thing for most children, but going in a pool had always been Jared's dream. "It feels great!" he yelled. He soon was up to his waist in the clear, turquoise water, splashing and shouting with joy. Alicia and David joined him, and together they spent two hours paddling and horsing around.

A few days later, Jared asked me, "Daddy, can we move here? I could go to school with the other kids."

"I'll try, Jared. But first we'll have to make a few trips here so we can make sure the air is always this clean."

A year later, when Jared was eleven, we made a return trip to Albuquerque. As before, Jared was able to breathe more freely in the cleaner air. We were so encouraged by this that we plan to rent an apartment there for three months next summer. Marlene will stay with Jared and Alicia to see if, over a longer period of time, Albuquerque continues to be the haven we've been searching for. If it is, we plan to move there permanently.

For the rest of that first vacation in Albuquerque, Jared went outside in his mask for about two hours every day. He always told us when he felt he had to come in. He could sense his limits, even in this relatively pure air.

While our three growing children played, Marlene and I lounged by the pool, watching them. For these brief hours, Jared was no longer a bubble boy. He was free. Sitting there, I remembered Dr. Wilson's words: "There may be many Jareds out there. . . . He's probably the only survivor. . . . I'm confident Jared will someday outgrow his illness."

Someday, Jared will run free.